THE ULTIMATE
AIR FRYER
COOKBOOK
FOR BEGINNERS 2024

**1900 Days of Easy, Delicious, and Low-Fat
Recipes for Healthier Living**

Dorothy Torres

Notice Of Disclaimer.

Please note that the information in this document is intended for educational and entertainment purposes only. Every effort has been made to provide accurate, up-to-date, reliable and complete information. No warranty of any kind is declared or implied. The reader acknowledges that the author does not engage in the provision of legal, financial, medical or professional advice. The content in this book has been obtained from a variety of sources. Please consult a licensed professional before attempting any of the techniques described in this book. By reading this document, the reader agrees that in no event shall the author be liable for any direct or indirect damages, including but not limited to errors, omissions or inaccuracies, resulting from the use of the information in this document.

CONTENTS

INTRODUCTION 1

Bread And Breakfast 3

Western Omelet 3
Seedy Bagels 3
Peach Fritters 3
Mixed Berry Muffins 4
Hole In One 4
Roasted Tomato And Cheddar Rolls 4
Healthy Granola 5
Coconut & Peanut Rice Cereal 5
Huevos Rancheros 5
Western Frittata 6
English Scones 6
Oat Bran Muffins 7
Breakfast Sausage Bites 7
Christmas Eggnog Bread 7
Smoked Salmon Croissant Sandwich 8
Strawberry Streusel Muffins 8
Walnut Pancake 8
Fluffy Vegetable Strata 9
Apple French Toast Sandwich 9
Egg & Bacon Pockets 9

Beef, Pork & Lamb Recipes 10

Lollipop Lamb Chops With Mint Pesto 10
Kielbasa Sausage With Pierogies And Caramelized Onions 10
Lamb Meatballs With Quick Tomato Sauce 11
Chicken Fried Steak 11
Coffee-rubbed Pork Tenderloin 12
Chile Con Carne Galette 12
Egg Stuffed Pork Meatballs 12
Ground Beef Calzones 13
Friendly Bbq Baby Back Ribs 13
Flank Steak With Chimichurri Sauce 13
Spicy Hoisin Bbq Pork Chops 14
Italian Sausage Rolls 14
Vietnamese Beef Lettuce Wraps 14
Mustard-crusted Rib-eye 15

Indian Fry Bread Tacos 15
Bacon, Blue Cheese And Pear Stuffed Pork Chops 16
Tex-mex Beef Carnitas 16
Kentucky-style Pork Tenderloin 16
Authentic Country-style Pork Ribs 17
Cheesy Mushroom-stuffed Pork Loins 17
Crunchy Fried Pork Loin Chops 17
Paprika Fried Beef 18
Oktoberfest Bratwursts 18
Kawaii Pork Roast 18
Rib Eye Cheesesteaks With Fried Onions 19
Citrus Pork Lettuce Wraps 19
Delicious Juicy Pork Meatballs 20
Barbecue Country-style Pork Ribs 20
Greek Pita Pockets 20
German-style Pork Patties 21

Fish And Seafood Recipes 21

Herby Prawn & Zucchini Bake 21
Classic Crab Cakes 21
Shrimp "scampi" 22
Holiday Lobster Salad 22
Spicy Fish Street Tacos With Sriracha Slaw 22
Herb-crusted Sole 23
Horseradish Crusted Salmon 23
Horseradish Tuna Croquettes 23
Masala Fish `n´ Chips 24
Miso-rubbed Salmon Fillets 24
Panko-breaded Cod Fillets 24
Yummy Salmon Burgers With Salsa Rosa 25
Mom´s Tuna Melt Toastie 25
Basil Mushroom & Shrimp Spaghetti 25
Baltimore Crab Cakes 26
Saucy Shrimp 26
Tilapia Teriyaki 26
Mahi Mahi With Cilantro-chili Butter 27
Stuffed Shrimp 27
Perfect Soft-shelled Crabs 28
Shrimp Po'boy With Remoulade Sauce 28
Lemon & Herb Crusted Salmon 28

Mediterranean Salmon Burgers 29
Coconut Shrimp With Plum Sauce 29
Quick Tuna Tacos 29
Flounder Fillets 29
Fish Sticks For Grown-ups 30
Shrimp, Chorizo And Fingerling Potatoes 30
Fish Goujons With Tartar Sauce 31
Sweet Potato–wrapped Shrimp 31

Poultry Recipes 32

Mexican-inspired Chicken Breasts 32
Simple Buttermilk Fried Chicken 32
Chicken & Fruit Biryani 32
Intense Buffalo Chicken Wings 33
Taquitos 33
Spiced Chicken Breasts 33
Turkey Scotch Eggs 34
Tortilla Crusted Chicken Breast 34
Asian-style Orange Chicken 34
Super-simple Herby Turkey 35
Chicken Parmigiana 35
Indian Chicken Tandoori 35
Enchilada Chicken Quesadillas 36
Rich Turkey Burgers 36
Mexican Chicken Roll-ups 36
Classic Chicken Cobb Salad 37
Spinach & Turkey Meatballs 37
Buttered Chicken Thighs 37
Fiery Chicken Meatballs 38
Christmas Chicken & Roasted Grape Salad 38

Sandwiches And Burgers Recipes 39

Provolone Stuffed Meatballs 39
Sausage And Pepper Heros 39
Dijon Thyme Burgers 40
White Bean Veggie Burgers 40
Chicken Saltimbocca Sandwiches 41
Eggplant Parmesan Subs 41
Best-ever Roast Beef Sandwiches 41
Mexican Cheeseburgers 42
Chili Cheese Dogs 42
Reuben Sandwiches 43
Chicken Spiedies 43
Inside-out Cheeseburgers 44
Crunchy Falafel Balls 44

Black Bean Veggie Burgers 44
Salmon Burgers 45
Philly Cheesesteak Sandwiches 45
Asian Glazed Meatballs 46
Lamb Burgers 46
Chicken Apple Brie Melt 47
Chicken Gyros 47

Appetizers And Snacks 48

Caponata Salsa 48
Cheesy Pigs In A Blanket 48
Crispy Chicken Bites With Gorgonzola Sauce 49
Cheddar-pimiento Strips | Prep Time: 15 Minutes | Servings: 4 49
Corn Dog Bites 49
Popcorn Chicken Bites 50
Hot Cauliflower Bites 50
Brie-currant & Bacon Spread 50
Sweet Potato Fries With Sweet And Spicy Dipping Sauce 51
Fried Goat Cheese 51
Sweet-and-salty Pretzels 51
Dill Fried Pickles With Light Ranch Dip 52
Tempura Fried Veggies 52
Indian Cauliflower Tikka Bites 53
Mediterranean Potato Skins 53
Yellow Onion Rings 53
Orange-glazed Carrots 54
Homemade Pretzel Bites 54
Charred Shishito Peppers 55
Cheesy Tortellini Bites 55

Vegetable Side Dishes Recipes 56

Corn Au Gratin 56
Yellow Squash 56
Carrots & Parsnips With Tahini Sauce 56
Mini Hasselback Potatoes 57
Florentine Stuffed Tomatoes 57
Simple Peppared Carrot Chips 57
Sweet Potato Curly Fries 58
Brown Rice And Goat Cheese Croquettes 58
Veggie Fritters 58
Buttered Brussels Sprouts 59
Caraway Seed Pretzel Sticks 59
Baked Shishito Peppers 59

Southern Okra Chips 59
Home Fries 60
Sweet Potato Puffs 60
Chicken Eggrolls 61
Succulent Roasted Peppers 61
Roasted Herbed Shiitake Mushrooms 61
Stunning Apples & Onions 61
Cheesy Texas Toast 62

Vegetarian Recipes 63

Black Bean Empanadas 63
Spinach And Cheese Calzone 63
Parmesan Portobello Mushroom Caps 64
Vegan Buddha Bowls 64
Golden Breaded Mushrooms 64
Tacos 65
Party Giant Nachos 65
Quinoa Green Pizza 65
Bite-sized Blooming Onions 66
Black Bean Stuffed Potato Boats 66
Garlicky Brussel Sprouts With Saffron Aioli 66
Thyme Meatless Patties 67
Fake Shepherd´s Pie 67
Veggie Fried Rice 67
Quick-to-make Quesadillas 68
Vietnamese Gingered Tofu 68
Mushroom-rice Stuffed Bell Peppers 69
Asparagus, Mushroom And Cheese Soufflés 69

Spaghetti Squash And Kale Fritters With Pomodoro Sauce 69
Pizza Margherita With Spinach 70

Desserts And Sweets 71

German Streusel-stuffed Baked Apples 71
Oreo-coated Peanut Butter Cups 71
Home-style Pumpkin Pie Pudding 71
Fried Oreos Recipes 72
Fried Cannoli Wontons 72
Apple Dumplings 72
Honey-pecan Yogurt Cake 73
Baked Stuffed Pears 73
Wild Blueberry Sweet Empanadas 73
Cinnamon Tortilla Crisps 74
Sea-salted Caramel Cookie Cups 74
Roasted Pears 74
Cinnamon Canned Biscuit Donuts 75
Healthy Chickpea Cookies 75
Easy Churros 75
Cheesecake Wontons 76
Holiday Peppermint Cake 76
Fried Pineapple Chunks 76
Keto Cheesecake Cups 77
Kiwi Pastry Bites 77

INDEX 78

INTRODUCTION

⭐ ⭐ ⭐ The Ultimate Air Fryer Cookbook for Beginners 2024: 1900 Days of Easy, Delicious, and Low-Fat Recipes for Healthier Living ⭐ ⭐ ⭐

Are you ready to revolutionize your cooking and embark on a journey to healthier, tastier meals?

Looking for an extensive collection of air fryer recipes that are both easy to make and delicious?

Want to enjoy your favorite fried foods with less guilt and more nutrition?

If you answered YES to any of these questions, then "The Ultimate Air Fryer Cookbook for Beginners 2024" is your perfect kitchen companion!

✅ What You'll Find Inside:

🔍 1900 Days of Mouthwatering Recipes: From crispy appetizers to succulent main courses and guilt-free desserts, this cookbook has you covered for more than 5 years of daily cooking inspiration!

🍲 Low-Fat, Healthier Alternatives: Enjoy all your favorite fried foods with up to 75% less oil, without compromising on taste or texture.

👨‍🍳🔍 Beginner-Friendly Instructions: Step-by-step guides ensure even novice cooks can create restaurant-quality meals with ease.

🕐 Time-Saving Techniques: Quick and efficient recipes perfect for busy lifestyles.

💡 Expert Tips and Tricks: Master your air fryer with insider knowledge to get the most out of your appliance.

🛒 Easy-to-Find Ingredients: No obscure items – just simple, accessible ingredients for fuss-free cooking.

Discover a World of Flavors:

- 🍗 Crispy and Juicy Poultry Dishes

- 🥩 Perfectly Cooked Beef, Pork, and Lamb

- 🐟 Flaky and Delicious Fish and Seafood

- 🥦 Crisp and Flavorful Vegetables

- 🥪 Irresistible Snacks and Appetizers

- 🍰 Guilt-Free Desserts and Baked Goods

Whether you're a health-conscious foodie, a busy parent, or simply looking to expand your culinary horizons, this cookbook is your ticket to healthier, easier, and more delicious meals.

🎉 🎉 🎉 Don't Wait! Click "Buy Now" and Transform Your Cooking Today! 🎉 🎉 🎉

Start your journey to healthier living without sacrificing flavor. With "The Ultimate Air Fryer Cookbook for Beginners 2024," you'll be amazed at what you can create in your air fryer!

Bread And Breakfast

Western Omelet

Servings: 2 | Prep Time: 5 Minutes | Cooking Time: 22 Minutes

Ingredients:

- ¼ cup chopped onion
- ¼ cup chopped bell pepper, green or red
- ¼ cup diced ham
- 1 teaspoon butter
- 4 large eggs
- 2 tablespoons milk
- ⅛ teaspoon salt
- ¾ cup grated sharp Cheddar cheese

Directions:

1. Place onion, bell pepper, ham, and butter in air fryer baking pan. Cook at 200°C/390°F for 1 minute and stir.
2. Continue cooking 5 minutes, until vegetables are tender.
3. Beat together eggs, milk, and salt. Pour over vegetables and ham in baking pan.
4. Cook at 180°C/360°F for 15 minutes or until eggs set and top has browned slightly.
5. Sprinkle grated cheese on top of omelet. Cook 1 minute or just long enough to melt the cheese.

Variations & Ingredients Tips:

- Add cooked bacon, sauteed mushrooms or spinach to the veggie mix.
- Use pepper jack or Swiss cheese instead of cheddar.
- Serve with salsa, avocado or hot sauce on the side.

Per Serving: Calories: 390; Total Fat: 26g; Saturated Fat: 13g; Cholesterol: 430mg; Sodium: 920mg; Total Carbs: 8g; Dietary Fiber: 1g; Total Sugars: 4g; Protein: 29g

Seedy Bagels

Servings: 4 | Prep Time: 10 Minutes | Cooking Time: 25 Minutes

Ingredients:

- 1 ¼ cups flour
- 2 tsp baking powder
- ½ tsp salt
- 1 cup plain Greek yogurt
- 1 egg
- 1 tsp water
- 1 tsp poppy seeds
- ½ tsp white sesame seeds
- ½ tsp black sesame seeds
- ½ tsp coriander seeds
- 1 tsp cumin powder
- ½ tsp dried minced onion
- 1 tsp coarse salt

Directions:

1. Preheat air fryer to 150°C/300°F.
2. Mix 1 cup flour, baking powder, salt, and cumin.
3. Stir in yogurt to form a dough. Divide into 4.
4. Roll each into a 15-cm log and form into a bagel shape.
5. Whisk egg and water.
6. Make topping with seeds, onion and salt.
7. Brush bagels with egg wash and coat with topping mix.
8. Air fry 12-15 mins until golden brown.

Variations & Ingredients Tips:

- Use different seeds like flax, chia or everything bagel seasoning.
- Add dried fruit or nuts to the dough.
- Brush with egg white only for a vegan option.

Per Serving: Calories: 288; Total Fat: 5g; Saturated Fat: 1g; Cholesterol: 53mg; Sodium: 1043mg; Total Carbs: 50g; Dietary Fiber: 3g; Total Sugars: 4g; Protein: 11g

Peach Fritters

Servings: 8 | Prep Time: 30 Minutes | Cooking Time: 6 Minutes

Ingredients:

- 1½ cups bread flour
- 1 tsp active dry yeast
- ¼ cup sugar
- ¼ tsp salt
- ½ cup warm milk
- ½ tsp vanilla extract
- 2 egg yolks
- 2 tbsp melted butter
- 2 cups small diced peaches (fresh or frozen)
- 1 tbsp butter
- 1 tsp ground cinnamon
- 1 to 2 tbsp sugar
- Glaze
- ¾ cup powdered sugar
- 4 tsp milk

Directions:

1. Combine the flour, yeast, sugar and salt in a bowl. Add the milk, vanilla, egg yolks and melted butter and combine until the dough starts to come together.
2. Transfer the dough to a floured surface and knead it by hand for 2 minutes. Shape into a ball, place in a large oiled bowl, cover and let rise for 1 to 1½ hours.
3. Melt 1 tbsp butter in a saucepan. Add peaches, cinnamon and sugar. Cook for 5 minutes until softened. Set aside to cool.
4. When dough has risen, shape into a 30-cm circle. Spread peaches over half and fold other half over. Score in a diamond pattern cutting through top layer only.
5. Roll up from one end into an 20-cm log. Cut into 8 slices and place on floured sheet. Let rise 30 minutes.
6. Preheat air fryer to 190°C/370°F.

7. Air-fry 2-3 fritters at a time for 3 minutes. Flip and fry 2-3 minutes more until golden.
8. Make glaze by whisking powdered sugar and milk. Let fritters cool 10 minutes then glaze.

Variations & Ingredients Tips:

- Use other fruit like apples or berries instead of peaches.
- Add spices like cinnamon or nutmeg to the dough.
- Drizzle with a vanilla glaze instead.

Per Serving: Calories: 280; Total Fat: 7g; Saturated Fat: 3.6g; Cholesterol: 75mg; Sodium: 145mg; Total Carbohydrates: 48g; Dietary Fiber: 2g; Total Sugars: 18g; Protein: 5g

Mixed Berry Muffins

Servings: 8 | Prep Time: 15 Minutes | Cooking Time:12 To 17 Minutes

Ingredients:

- 1/3 cups plus 1 tablespoon all-purpose flour, divided
- 1/4 cup granulated sugar
- 2 tablespoons light brown sugar
- 2 teaspoons baking powder
- 2 eggs
- 2/3 cup whole milk
- 1/3 cup safflower oil
- 1 cup mixed fresh berries

Directions:

1. In a medium bowl, stir together 1/3 cups of flour, the granulated sugar, brown sugar, and bak-ing powder until mixed well.
2. In a small bowl, whisk the eggs, milk, and oil until combined. Stir the egg mixture into the dry ingredients just until combined.
3. In another small bowl, toss the mixed berries with the remaining 1 tablespoon of flour until coated. Gently stir the berries into the batter.
4. Double up 16 foil muffincups to make 8 cups.
5. Insert the crisper plate into the basket and the basket into the unit. Preheat the unit by selecting BAKE, setting the temperature to 155°C/315°F, and set-ting the time to 3 minutes. Select START/STOP to begin.
6. Once the unit is preheated, place 4 cups into the basket and fill each three-quarters full with the batter.
7. Select BAKE, set the temperature to 155°C/315°F, and set the time for 17 minutes. Select START/STOP to begin.
8. After about 12 minutes, check the muffins. If they spring back when lightly touched with your finger, they are done. If not, resume cooking.
9. When the cooking is done, transfer the mu fins to a wire rack to cool.
10. Repeat steps 6, 7, and 8 with the remaining muffin cups and batter.
11. Let the muffins cool for 10 minutes before serving.

Variations & Ingredients Tips:

- Toss the berries with a bit of flour before folding into the batter to prevent them from sinking.
- Fill muffin cups almost to the top as they won't rise much in the air fryer.
- Check for doneness a few minutes early by gently pressing the tops - they should spring back when done.

Per Serving: Calories: 230; Cholesterol: 43mg; Total Fat: 11g; Saturated Fat: 2g; Sodium: 126mg; Total Carbohydrates: 30g; Dietary Fiber: 1g; Total Sugars: 12g; Protein: 4g

Hole In One

Servings: 1 | Prep Time: 5 Minutes | Cooking Time: 7 Minutes

Ingredients:

- 1 slice bread
- 1 teaspoon soft butter
- 1 egg
- salt and pepper
- 1 tablespoon shredded Cheddar cheese
- 2 teaspoons diced ham

Directions:

1. Place a 15 x 15 cm baking dish inside air fryer basket and preheat fryer to 165°C/330°F.
2. Using a 6.4 cm-diameter biscuit cutter, cut a hole in center of bread slice.
3. Spread softened butter on both sides of bread.
4. Lay bread slice in baking dish and crack egg into the hole. Sprinkle egg with salt and pepper to taste.
5. Cook for 5 minutes.
6. Turn toast over and top it with shredded cheese and diced ham.
7. Cook for 2 more minutes or until yolk is done to your liking.

Variations & Ingredients Tips:

- Use bagels, English muffins or biscuits instead of bread.
- Add some sliced avocado, smoked salmon or sautéed spinach on top.
- Sprinkle with everything bagel seasoning or chopped chives for extra flavor.

Per Serving: Calories: 293; Total Fat: 18g; Saturated Fat: 8g; Cholesterol: 215mg; Sodium: 569mg; Total Carbs: 19g; Dietary Fiber: 1g; Total Sugars: 2g; Protein: 14g

Roasted Tomato And Cheddar Rolls

Servings: 12 | Prep Time: 30 Minutes | Cooking Time: 55 Minutes

Ingredients:

- 4 Roma tomatoes
- ½ clove garlic, minced
- 1 tbsp olive oil
- ¼ tsp dried thyme

- Salt and pepper to taste
- 4 cups all-purpose flour
- 1 tsp active dry yeast
- 2 tsp sugar
- 2 tsp salt
- 1 tbsp olive oil
- 1 cup grated Cheddar cheese, plus more for sprinkling at the end
- 1½ cups water

Directions:

1. Toss tomatoes with garlic, 1 tbsp olive oil, thyme, salt and pepper.
2. Preheat air fryer to 200°C/390°F.
3. Air fry tomatoes cut-side up for 10 mins, shake, then 5-10 more mins at 165°C/330°F until no longer juicy. Cool and chop.
4. Mix flour, yeast, sugar, salt. Add 1 tbsp oil, tomatoes, cheese and knead with 1¼ cups water for 10 mins, adding more water as needed.
5. Let dough rise 1-2 hours. Divide into 12, roll into balls. Let rest 45 mins.
6. Preheat to 180°C/360°F. Spray dough balls and basket with oil.
7. Air fry 3 rolls at a time for 10 mins, adding cheese on top the last 2 mins.

Variations & Ingredients Tips:

- Add dried herbs, garlic or onions to the dough.
- Brush with egg wash before baking for a glossy finish.
- Fill with cheese, pesto or other fillings before rolling.

Per Serving: Calories: 274; Total Fat: 8g; Saturated Fat: 3g; Cholesterol: 14mg; Sodium: 501mg; Total Carbs: 42g; Dietary Fiber: 2g; Total Sugars: 2g; Protein: 8g

Healthy Granola

Servings: 4 | Prep Time: 10 Minutes | Cooking Time: 10 Minutes

Ingredients:

- 59 ml chocolate hazelnut spread
- 1 cup chopped pecans
- 1 cup quick-cooking oats
- 1 tablespoon chia seeds
- 1 tablespoon flaxseed
- 1 tablespoon sesame seeds
- 1 cup coconut shreds
- 59 ml maple syrup
- 1 tablespoon light brown sugar
- ½ teaspoon vanilla extract
- 28 g hazelnut flour
- 2 tablespoons cocoa powder
- Salt to taste

Directions:

1. Preheat air fryer at 175°C/350°F. Combine the pecans, oats, chia seeds, flaxseed, sesame seeds, coconut shreds, chocolate hazelnut spread, maple syrup, sugar, vanilla extract, hazelnut flour, cocoa powder, and salt in a bowl. Press mixture into a greased cake pan. Place cake pan in the frying basket and Bake for 5 minutes, stirring once. Let

cool completely before crumbling. Store it into an airtight container up to 5 days.

Variations & Ingredients Tips:

- Use honey, agave or date syrup instead of maple syrup for different sweetness.
- Add some dried fruits like raisins, cranberries or apricots after baking.
- Serve with yogurt, milk or sprinkled over smoothie bowls or ice cream.

Per Serving: Calories: 642; Total Fat: 43g; Saturated Fat: 16g; Cholesterol: 0mg; Sodium: 117mg; Total Carbs: 59g; Dietary Fiber: 10g; Total Sugars: 31g; Protein: 11g

Coconut & Peanut Rice Cereal

Servings: 4 | Prep Time: 5 Minutes | Cooking Time: 15 Minutes

Ingredients:

- 4 cups rice cereal
- 1 cup coconut shreds
- 2 tablespoons peanut butter
- 1 teaspoon vanilla extract
- ¼ cup honey
- 1 tablespoon light brown sugar
- 2 teaspoons ground cinnamon
- ¼ cup hazelnut flour
- Salt to taste

Directions:

1. Preheat air fryer at 180°C/350°F.
2. Combine the rice cereal, coconut shreds, peanut butter, vanilla extract, honey, brown sugar, cinnamon, hazelnut flour, and salt in a bowl.
3. Press mixture into a greased cake pan. Place cake pan in the frying basket and Air Fry for 5 minutes, stirring once.
4. Let cool completely for 10 minutes before crumbling.
5. Store it into an airtight container up to 5 days.

Variations & Ingredients Tips:

- Use different types of cereal, such as corn flakes or wheat bran, for a variety of flavors and textures.
- Add some dried fruit, such as raisins or cranberries, for extra sweetness.
- For a nut-free version, replace the peanut butter and hazelnut flour with sunflower seed butter and oat flour.

Per Serving: Calories: 360; Total Fat: 14g; Saturated Fat: 9g; Cholesterol: 0mg; Sodium: 180mg; Total Carbs: 57g; Fiber: 3g; Sugars: 30g; Protein: 5g

Huevos Rancheros

Servings: 4 | Prep Time: 10 Minutes | Cooking Time: 45 Minutes + Cooling Time

Ingredients:

- 1 tablespoon olive oil
- 20 cherry tomatoes, halved
- 2 chopped plum tomatoes
- 59 ml tomato sauce
- 2 scallions, sliced
- 2 garlic cloves, minced
- 1 teaspoon honey
- ½ teaspoon salt
- ⅛ teaspoon cayenne pepper
- ¼ teaspoon grated nutmeg
- ¼ teaspoon paprika
- 4 eggs

Directions:

1. Preheat the air fryer to 190°C/370°F. Combine the olive oil, cherry tomatoes, plum tomatoes, tomato sauce, scallions, garlic, nutmeg, honey, salt, paprika and cayenne in an 18 cm springform pan that has been wrapped in foil to prevent leaks. Put the pan in the frying basket and Bake the mix for 15-20 minutes, stirring twice until the tomatoes are soft. Mash some of the tomatoes in the pan with a fork, then stir them into the sauce. Also, break the eggs into the sauce, then return the pan to the fryer and Bake for 2 minutes. Remove the pan from the fryer and stir the eggs into the sauce, whisking them through the sauce. Don't mix in completely. Cook for 4-8 minutes more or until the eggs are set. Let cool, then serve.

Variations & Ingredients Tips:

- Serve with warm corn tortillas, refried beans and sliced avocado.
- Top with crumbled queso fresco or cotija cheese.
- Add some chopped jalapeños or chipotle peppers for extra heat.

Per Serving: Calories: 164; Total Fat: 11g; Saturated Fat: 3g; Cholesterol: 186mg; Sodium: 425mg; Total Carbs: 10g; Dietary Fiber: 2g; Total Sugars: 6g; Protein: 8g

Western Frittata

Servings: 1 | Prep Time: 10 Minutes | Cooking Time: 19 Minutes

Ingredients:

- ½ red or green bell pepper, cut into 1.3cm chunks
- 1 teaspoon olive oil
- 3 eggs, beaten
- ¼ cup grated Cheddar cheese
- ¼ cup diced cooked ham
- salt and freshly ground black pepper, to taste
- 1 teaspoon butter
- 1 teaspoon chopped fresh parsley

Directions:

1. Preheat the air fryer to 200°C/400°F.
2. Toss the peppers with the olive oil and air-fry for 6 minutes, shaking the basket once or twice during the cooking process to redistribute the ingredients.
3. While the vegetables are cooking, beat the eggs well in a

bowl, stir in the Cheddar cheese and ham, and season with salt and freshly ground black pepper. Add the air-fried peppers to this bowl when they have finished cooking.

4. Place a 15cm or 18cm non-stick metal cake pan into the air fryer basket with the butter using an aluminum sling to lower the pan into the basket. (Fold a piece of aluminum foil into a strip about 5cm wide by 60cm long.)
5. Air-fry for 1 minute at 190°C/380°F to melt the butter. Remove the cake pan and rotate the pan to distribute the butter and grease the pan. Pour the egg mixture into the cake pan and return the pan to the air fryer, using the aluminum sling.
6. Air-fry at 190°C/380°F for 12 minutes, or until the frittata has puffed up and is lightly browned. Let the frittata sit in the air fryer for 5 minutes to cool to an edible temperature and set up. Remove the cake pan from the air fryer, sprinkle with parsley and serve immediately.

Variations & Ingredients Tips:

- Add sauteed mushrooms, spinach or other veggies to the egg mixture.
- Use feta or goat cheese instead of cheddar.
- Serve with salsa, avocado or hot sauce on top.

Per Serving: Calories: 435; Total Fat: 29g; Saturated Fat: 11g; Cholesterol: 535mg; Sodium: 865mg; Total Carbs: 7g; Dietary Fiber: 1g; Total Sugars: 3g; Protein: 33g

English Scones

Servings: 8 | Prep Time: 15 Minutes | Cooking Time: 8 Minutes

Ingredients:

- 2 cups all-purpose flour
- 1 tablespoon baking powder
- ½ teaspoon salt
- 2 tablespoons sugar
- ¼ cup unsalted butter
- 158 ml plus 15 ml whole milk, divided

Directions:

1. Preheat the air fryer to 190°C/380°F.
2. In a large bowl, whisk together the flour, baking powder, salt, and sugar. Using a pastry blender or your fingers, cut in the butter until pea-size crumbles appear. Make a well in the center and pour in 158 ml of the milk. Quickly mix the batter until a ball forms. Knead the dough 3 times.
3. Place the dough onto a floured surface and, using your hands or a rolling pin, flatten the dough until it's 2 cm thick. Using a biscuit cutter or drinking glass, cut out 10 circles, reforming the dough and flattening as needed to use up the batter.
4. Brush the tops lightly with the remaining 15 ml of milk.
5. Place the scones into the air fryer basket. Cook for 8 minutes or until golden brown and cooked in the center.

Variations & Ingredients Tips:

- Add some dried currants, chocolate chips or chopped candied ginger to the dough.
- Sprinkle the tops with coarse sugar or brush with cream before baking.
- Serve with clotted cream, lemon curd or your favorite jam.

Per Serving: Calories: 218; Total Fat: 8g; Saturated Fat: 5g; Cholesterol: 21mg; Sodium: 292mg; Total Carbs: 32g; Dietary Fiber: 1g; Total Sugars: 4g; Protein: 5g

Oat Bran Muffins

Servings: 8 | Prep Time: 10 Minutes | Cooking Time: 12 Minutes

Ingredients:

- ⅔ cup oat bran
- ½ cup flour
- ¼ cup brown sugar
- 1 tsp baking powder
- ½ tsp baking soda
- ⅛ tsp salt
- ½ cup buttermilk
- 1 egg
- 2 tbsp canola oil
- ½ cup chopped dates, raisins, or dried cranberries
- 24 paper muffin cups
- Cooking spray

Directions:

1. Preheat air fryer to 165°C/330°F.
2. In a large bowl, combine the oat bran, flour, brown sugar, baking powder, baking soda, and salt.
3. In a small bowl, beat together the buttermilk, egg, and oil.
4. Pour buttermilk mixture into bowl with dry ingredients and stir just until moistened. Do not beat.
5. Gently stir in dried fruit.
6. Use triple baking cups to help muffins hold shape during baking. Spray them with cooking spray, place 4 sets of cups in air fryer basket at a time, and fill each one ¾ full of batter.
7. Cook for 12 minutes, until top springs back when lightly touched and toothpick inserted in center comes out clean.
8. Repeat for remaining muffins.

Variations & Ingredients Tips:

- Add nuts, chocolate chips, or diced fruit to the batter.
- Replace buttermilk with milk or plant-based milk.
- Sprinkle with streusel or glaze topping before baking.

Per Serving: Calories: 106; Total Fat: 3g; Saturated Fat: 0.4g; Cholesterol: 18mg; Sodium: 126mg; Total Carbohydrates: 18g; Dietary Fiber: 2.3g; Total Sugars: 8.3g; Protein: 2.5g

Breakfast Sausage Bites

Servings: 4 | Prep Time: 10 Minutes | Cooking Time: 30 Minutes

Ingredients:

- 454g ground pork sausages
- ¼ cup diced onions
- 1 tsp rubbed sage
- ¼ tsp ground nutmeg
- ½ tsp fennel seeds
- ¼ tsp garlic powder
- 2 tbsp parsley, chopped
- Salt and pepper to taste

Directions:

1. Preheat air fryer at 177°C/350°F.
2. Combine all ingredients except parsley in a bowl.
3. Form mixture into balls.
4. Place balls in a greased air fryer basket.
5. Air fry for 10 minutes, flipping once halfway.
6. Sprinkle with parsley and serve immediately.

Variations & Ingredients Tips:

- Use turkey or chicken sausage for less fat.
- Add shredded cheese or diced peppers to the mixture.
- Serve with maple syrup or honey mustard for dipping.

Per Serving: Calories: 400; Total Fat: 32g; Saturated Fat: 12g; Cholesterol: 80mg; Sodium: 630mg; Total Carbs: 4g; Dietary Fiber: 1g; Total Sugars: 1g; Protein: 21g

Christmas Eggnog Bread

Servings: 6 | Prep Time: 10 Minutes | Cooking Time: 18 Minutes

Ingredients:

- 1 cup flour, plus more for dusting
- ¼ cup sugar
- 1 teaspoon baking powder
- ¼ teaspoon salt
- ¼ teaspoon nutmeg
- ½ cup eggnog
- 1 egg yolk
- 1 tablespoon butter, plus 1 teaspoon, melted
- ¼ cup pecans
- ¼ cup chopped candied fruit (cherries, pineapple, or mixed fruits)
- Cooking spray

Directions:

1. Preheat air fryer to 180°C/360°F.
2. In a medium bowl, stir together the flour, sugar, baking powder, salt, and nutmeg.
3. Add eggnog, egg yolk, and butter. Mix well but do not beat.
4. Stir in nuts and fruit.
5. Spray a 15 x 15 cm baking pan with cooking spray and dust with flour.
6. Spread batter into prepared pan and cook at 180°C/360°F for 18 minutes or until top is dark golden brown and bread starts to pull away from sides of pan.

Variations & Ingredients Tips:

- Use different types of nuts, such as walnuts or almonds, for a variety of flavors and textures.
- Add some grated orange or lemon zest to the batter for

- extra flavor.
- For a boozier version, replace some of the eggnog with rum or bourbon.

Per Serving: Calories: 230; Total Fat: 9g; Saturated Fat: 3.5g; Cholesterol: 45mg; Sodium: 220mg; Total Carbs: 32g; Fiber: 1g; Sugars: 14g; Protein: 4g

Smoked Salmon Croissant Sandwich

Servings: 1 | Prep Time: 5 Minutes | Cooking Time: 30 Minutes

Ingredients:

- 1 croissant, halved
- 2 eggs
- 1 tbsp guacamole
- 1 smoked salmon slice
- Salt and pepper to taste

Directions:

1. Preheat air fryer to 180°C/360°F.
2. Place croissant halves in basket, crusty side up. Whisk eggs and place in fryer.
3. Bake 10 mins. Gently scramble eggs. Flip croissant and cook 10 more mins until eggs cooked.
4. Place one croissant half on plate, spread with guacamole.
5. Top with scrambled eggs, then salmon.
6. Sprinkle with salt and pepper. Top with other croissant half.
7. Serve hot.

Variations & Ingredients Tips:

- Use different croissant flavors like chocolate or almond.
- Substitute cream cheese or avocado spread for guacamole.
- Add caramelized onions, spinach or tomatoes.

Per Serving: Calories: 462; Total Fat: 29g; Saturated Fat: 11g; Cholesterol: 386mg; Sodium: 798mg; Total Carbs: 34g; Dietary Fiber: 2g; Total Sugars: 5g; Protein: 19g

Strawberry Streusel Muffins

Servings: 12 | Prep Time: 15 Minutes | Cooking Time: 14 Minutes

Ingredients:

- 1¾ cups all-purpose flour
- ½ cup granulated sugar
- 2 tsp baking powder
- ¼ tsp baking soda
- ½ tsp salt
- ½ cup plain yogurt
- ½ cup milk
- ¼ cup vegetable oil
- 2 large eggs
- 1 tsp vanilla extract
- ½ cup freeze-dried strawberries
- 2 tbsp brown sugar
- ¼ cup oats
- 2 tbsp butter

Directions:

1. Preheat air fryer to 165°C/330°F.
2. Whisk flour, sugar, baking powder, soda and salt in one bowl.
3. Whisk yogurt, milk, oil, eggs and vanilla in another bowl.
4. Make a well and pour wet into dry, mix 1 min until lumpy. Fold in strawberries.
5. Mix brown sugar, oats and butter for streusel topping.
6. Fill 6 muffin liners 2/3 full. Top with half the streusel.
7. Bake 14 mins until a toothpick comes out clean. Repeat with remaining batter/topping.
8. Serve warm.

Variations & Ingredients Tips:

- Use fresh or frozen berries instead of freeze-dried.
- Add lemon or orange zest to the batter.
- Top with a cream cheese or vanilla glaze.

Per Serving: Calories: 211; Total Fat: 8g; Saturated Fat: 2g; Cholesterol: 39mg; Sodium: 196mg; Total Carbs: 31g; Dietary Fiber: 1g; Total Sugars: 14g; Protein: 4g

Walnut Pancake

Servings: 4 | Prep Time: 10 Minutes | Cooking Time: 20 Minutes

Ingredients:

- 3 tablespoons butter, divided into thirds
- 1 cup flour
- 1½ teaspoons baking powder
- ¼ teaspoon salt
- 2 tablespoons sugar
- ¾ cup milk
- 1 egg, beaten
- 1 teaspoon pure vanilla extract
- ½ cup walnuts, roughly chopped
- maple syrup or fresh sliced fruit, for serving

Directions:

1. Place 1 tablespoon of the butter in air fryer baking pan. Cook at 165°C/330°F for 3 minutes to melt.
2. In a small dish or pan, melt the remaining 2 tablespoons of butter either in the microwave or on the stove.
3. In a medium bowl, stir together the flour, baking powder, salt, and sugar. Add milk, beaten egg, the 2 tablespoons of melted butter, and vanilla. Stir until combined but do not beat. Batter may be slightly lumpy.
4. Pour batter over the melted butter in air fryer baking pan. Sprinkle nuts evenly over top.
5. Cook for 20 minutes or until toothpick inserted in center comes out clean. Turn air fryer off, close the machine, and let pancake rest for 2 minutes.
6. Remove pancake from pan, slice, and serve with syrup or fresh fruit.

Variations & Ingredients Tips:

- Substitute different nuts like pecans or almonds for the walnuts.

- Add chocolate chips, berries or banana slices to the batter.
- Top with powdered sugar or whipped cream instead of syrup.

Per Serving: Calories: 300; Total Fat: 17g; Saturated Fat: 6g; Cholesterol: 60mg; Sodium: 290mg; Total Carbs: 32g; Dietary Fiber: 2g; Total Sugars: 8g; Protein: 7g

Fluffy Vegetable Strata

Servings: 4 | Prep Time: 15 Minutes | Cooking Time: 30 Minutes

Ingredients:

- ½ red onion, thickly sliced
- 8 asparagus, sliced
- 1 baby carrot, shredded
- 227 g mushrooms, sliced
- ½ red bell pepper, chopped
- 2 bread slices, cubed
- 3 eggs
- 3 tablespoons milk
- 113 g mozzarella cheese
- 2 teaspoons chives, chopped

Directions:

1. Preheat air fryer to 165°C/330°F. Add the red onion, asparagus, carrots, mushrooms, red bell pepper, mushrooms, and 15 ml of water to a baking pan. Put it in the air fryer and Bake for 3-5 minutes, until crispy. Remove the pan, add the bread cubes, and shake to mix. Combine the eggs, milk, and chives and pour them over the veggies. Cover with mozzarella cheese. Bake for 12-15 minutes. The strata should puff up and set, while the top should be brown. Serve hot.

Variations & Ingredients Tips:

- Use different veggies like spinach, zucchini, tomatoes or broccoli based on preference.
- Swap mozzarella for cheddar, Swiss or feta cheese.
- Add some cooked sausage, bacon or ham for a meaty version.

Per Serving: Calories: 232; Total Fat: 12g; Saturated Fat: 6g; Cholesterol: 161mg; Sodium: 314mg; Total Carbs: 16g; Dietary Fiber: 2g; Total Sugars: 5g; Protein: 16g

Apple French Toast Sandwich

Servings: 1 | Prep Time: 10 Minutes | Cooking Time: 30 Minutes

Ingredients:

- 2 white bread slices
- 2 eggs
- 1 tsp cinnamon
- ½ peeled apple, sliced
- 1 tbsp brown sugar
- ¼ cup whipped cream

Directions:

1. Preheat air fryer to 177°C/350°F. Coat the apple slices with brown sugar in a small bowl. Whisk the eggs and cinnamon into a separate bowl until fluffy and completely blended. Coat the bread slices with the egg mixture, then place them on the greased frying basket. Top with apple slices and Air Fry for 20 minutes, flipping once until the bread is browned nicely and the apple is crispy.
2. Place one French toast slice onto a serving plate, then spoon the whipped cream on top and spread evenly. Scoop the caramelized apple slices onto the whipped cream, and cover with the second toast slice. Serve.

Variations & Ingredients Tips:

- Use brioche or challah bread for extra richness
- Add crushed nuts or granola to the sandwich
- Drizzle with maple syrup before serving

Per Serving: Calories: 455; Total Fat: 19g; Saturated Fat: 10g; Cholesterol: 290mg; Sodium: 370mg; Total Carbs: 62g; Dietary Fiber: 4g; Total Sugars: 28g; Protein: 13g

Egg & Bacon Pockets

Servings: 4 | Prep Time: 30 Minutes | Cooking Time: 50 Minutes

Ingredients:

- 2 tablespoons olive oil
- 4 bacon slices, chopped
- ¼ red bell pepper, diced
- 1/3 cup scallions, chopped
- 4 eggs, beaten
- 1/3 cup grated Swiss cheese
- 1 cup flour
- 1½ teaspoons baking powder
- ½ teaspoon salt
- 1 cup Greek yogurt
- 1 egg white, beaten
- 2 teaspoons Italian seasoning
- 1 tablespoon Tabasco sauce

Directions:

1. Warm the olive oil in a skillet over medium heat and add the bacon. Stir-fry for 3-4 minutes or until crispy. Add the bell pepper and scallions and sauté for 3-4 minutes. Pour in the beaten eggs and stir-fry to scramble them, 3 minutes. Stir in the Swiss cheese and set aside to cool.
2. Sift the flour, baking powder, and salt in a bowl. Add yogurt and mix together until combined. Transfer the dough to a floured workspace. Knead it for 3 minutes or until smooth. Form the dough into 4 equal balls. Roll out the balls into round discs. Divide the bacon-egg mixture between the rounds. Fold the dough over the filling and seal the edges with a fork. Brush the pockets with egg white and sprinkle with Italian seasoning.
3. Preheat air fryer to 175°C/350°F. Arrange the pockets on the greased frying basket and Bake for 9-11 minutes, flipping once until golden. Serve with Tabasco sauce.

Variations & Ingredients Tips:

- Use sausage, ham or smoked salmon instead of bacon.
- Add sautéed mushrooms, spinach or sun-dried tomatoes to the egg mixture.
- Serve with salsa, hot sauce or ketchup for dipping.

Per Serving: Calories: 468; Total Fat: 26g; Saturated Fat: 8g; Cholesterol: 225mg; Sodium: 826mg; Total Carbs: 36g; Dietary Fiber: 1g; Total Sugars: 4g; Protein: 23g

Beef, Pork & Lamb Recipes

Lollipop Lamb Chops With Mint Pesto

Servings: 4 | Prep Time: 20 Minutes | Cooking Time: 7 Minutes

Ingredients:

- Mint Pesto
- ½ small clove garlic
- ¼ cup packed fresh parsley
- ¾ cup packed fresh mint
- ½ teaspoon lemon juice
- ¼ cup grated Parmesan cheese
- 80 ml shelled pistachios
- ¼ teaspoon salt
- 120 ml olive oil
- 8 "frenched" lamb chops (1 rack)
- Olive oil
- Salt and freshly ground black pepper
- 1 tablespoon dried rosemary, chopped
- 1 tablespoon dried thyme

Directions:

1. Make the pesto by combining the garlic, parsley and mint in a food processor and process until finely chopped. Add the lemon juice, Parmesan cheese, pistachios and salt. Process until all the ingredients have turned into a paste. With the processor running, slowly pour the olive oil in through the feed tube. Scrape the sides of the processor with a spatula and process for another 30 seconds.
2. Preheat the air fryer to 200°C/400°F.
3. Rub both sides of the lamb chops with olive oil and season with salt, pepper, rosemary and thyme, pressing the herbs into the meat gently with your fingers. Transfer the lamb chops to the air fryer basket.
4. Air-fry the lamb chops at 200°C/400°F for 5 minutes. Flip the chops over and air-fry for an additional 2 minutes. This should bring the chops to a medium-rare doneness, depending on their thickness. Adjust the cooking time up or down a minute or two accordingly for different degrees of doneness.
5. Serve the lamb chops with mint pesto drizzled on top.

Variations & Ingredients Tips:

- Use different types of nuts, such as almonds or walnuts, for a variety of flavors and textures.
- Add some red pepper flakes or lemon zest to the pesto for

extra flavor.
- Serve the lamb chops with a side of roasted vegetables or couscous for a complete meal.

Per Serving: Calories: 730; Total Fat: 66g; Saturated Fat: 16g; Cholesterol: 95mg; Sodium: 470mg; Total Carbs: 5g; Fiber: 2g; Sugars: 1g; Protein: 31g

Kielbasa Sausage With Pierogies And Caramelized Onions

Servings: 3 | Prep Time: 10 Minutes | Cooking Time: 30 Minutes

Ingredients:

- 1 Vidalia or sweet onion, sliced
- Olive oil
- Salt and freshly ground black pepper
- 2 tablespoons butter, cut into small cubes
- 1 teaspoon sugar
- 454g light Polish kielbasa sausage, cut into 5cm chunks
- 1 (368g) package frozen mini pierogies
- 2 teaspoons vegetable or olive oil
- Chopped scallions

Directions:

1. Preheat the air fryer to 400°F/205°C.
2. Toss the sliced onions with a little olive oil, salt and pepper and transfer them to the air fryer basket. Dot the onions with pieces of butter and air-fry at 400°F/205°C for 2 minutes. Then sprinkle the sugar over the onions and stir. Pour any melted butter from the bottom of the air fryer drawer over the onions (do this over the sink – some of the butter will spill through the basket). Continue to air-fry for another 13 minutes, stirring or shaking the basket every few minutes to cook the onions evenly.
3. Add the kielbasa chunks to the onions and toss. Air-fry for another 5 minutes, shaking the basket halfway through the cooking time. Transfer the kielbasa and onions to a bowl and cover with aluminum foil to keep warm.
4. Toss the frozen pierogies with the vegetable or olive oil and transfer them to the air fryer basket. Air-fry at 400°F/205°C for 8 minutes, shaking the basket twice during the cooking

time.

5. When the pierogies have finished cooking, return the kielbasa and onions to the air fryer and gently toss with the pierogies. Air-fry for 2 more minutes and then transfer everything to a serving platter. Garnish with the chopped scallions and serve hot with the spicy sour cream sauce below.

Variations & Ingredients Tips:

● Use turkey or chicken kielbasa for a leaner option
● Substitute frozen potato pancakes or tater tots for the pierogies
● Top with sauteed mushrooms or shredded cheese

Per Serving: Calories: 740; Total Fat: 40g; Saturated Fat: 15g; Cholesterol: 90mg; Sodium: 1990mg; Total Carbs: 70g; Dietary Fiber: 5g; Total Sugars: 5g; Protein: 25g

Lamb Meatballs With Quick Tomato Sauce

Servings: 4 | Prep Time: 20 Minutes | Cooking Time: 8 Minutes

Ingredients:

- ½ small onion, finely diced
- 1 clove garlic, minced
- 450 g ground lamb
- 2 tablespoons fresh parsley, finely chopped (plus more for garnish)
- 2 teaspoons fresh oregano, finely chopped
- 2 tablespoons milk
- 1 egg yolk
- Salt and freshly ground black pepper

- ½ cup crumbled feta cheese, for garnish
- Tomato Sauce:
- 2 tablespoons butter
- 1 clove garlic, smashed
- Pinch crushed red pepper flakes
- ¼ teaspoon ground cinnamon
- 1 (800 g) can crushed tomatoes
- Salt, to taste

Directions:

1. Combine all ingredients for the meatballs in a large bowl and mix just until everything is combined. Shape the mixture into 4 cm balls or shape the meat between two spoons to make quenelles (little three-sided footballs).
2. Preheat the air fryer to 200°C/400°F.
3. While the air fryer is preheating, start the quick tomato sauce. Place the butter, garlic and red pepper flakes in a sauté pan and heat over medium heat on the stovetop. Let the garlic sizzle a little, but before the butter starts to brown, add the cinnamon and tomatoes. Bring to a simmer and simmer for 15 minutes. Season to taste with salt (but not too much as the feta that you will be sprinkling on at the end will be salty).
4. Brush the bottom of the air fryer basket with a little oil and transfer the meatballs to the air fryer basket in one layer,

air-frying in batches if necessary.

5. Air-fry at 200°C/400°F for 8 minutes, giving the basket a shake once during the cooking process to turn the meatballs over.
6. To serve, spoon a pool of the tomato sauce onto plates and add the meatballs in a decorative manner. Sprinkle the feta cheese on top and garnish with more fresh parsley. Serve immediately.

Variations & Ingredients Tips:

● Use different types of cheese, such as goat cheese or Parmesan, for a variety of flavors.
● Add some chopped Kalamata olives or capers to the tomato sauce for a briny flavor.
● Serve the meatballs with a side of pasta or crusty bread for a complete meal.

Per Serving: Calories: 510; Total Fat: 38g; Saturated Fat: 18g; Cholesterol: 170mg; Sodium: 780mg; Total Carbs: 15g; Fiber: 3g; Sugars: 8g; Protein: 31g

Chicken Fried Steak

Servings: 4 | Prep Time: 10 Minutes | Cooking Time: 15 Minutes

Ingredients:

- 2 eggs
- 1/2 cup buttermilk
- 1 1/2 cups flour
- 3/4 teaspoon salt
- 1/2 teaspoon pepper

- 450g beef cube steaks
- Salt and pepper
- Oil for misting or cooking spray

Directions:

1. Beat together eggs and buttermilk in a shallow dish.
2. In another shallow dish, stir together the flour, 1/2 teaspoon salt, and 1/4 teaspoon pepper.
3. Season cube steaks with remaining salt and pepper to taste. Dip in flour, buttermilk egg wash, and then flour again.
4. Spray both sides of steaks with oil or cooking spray.
5. Cooking in 2 batches, place steaks in air fryer basket in single layer. Cook at 360°F/182°C for 10 minutes. Spray tops of steaks with oil and cook 5 minutes or until meat is well done.
6. Repeat to cook remaining steaks.

Variations & Ingredients Tips:

● Use seasoned salt or Cajun seasoning in the flour dredge for extra flavor
● Substitute chicken or veggie broth for the buttermilk
● Top cooked steaks with pepper gravy or mushroom gravy

Per Serving: Calories: 390; Total Fat: 16g; Saturated Fat: 5g; Cholesterol: 165mg; Sodium: 550mg; Total Carbohydrates: 26g; Dietary Fiber: 1g; Total Sugars: 3g; Protein: 35g

Coffee-rubbed Pork Tenderloin

Servings: 4 | Prep Time: 10 Minutes | Cooking Time: 30 Minutes

Ingredients:

- 1 tablespoon packed brown sugar
- 2 teaspoons espresso powder
- 1 teaspoon bell pepper powder
- ½ teaspoon dried parsley
- 1 tablespoon honey
- ½ tablespoon lemon juice
- 2 teaspoons olive oil
- 450 g pork tenderloin

Directions:

1. Preheat air fryer to 200°C/400°F.
2. Toss the brown sugar, espresso powder, bell pepper powder, and parsley in a bowl and mix together. Add the honey, lemon juice, and olive oil, then stir well.
3. Smear the pork with the mix, then allow to marinate for 10 minutes before putting it in the air fryer.
4. Roast for 9-11 minutes until the pork is cooked through.
5. Slice before serving.

Variations & Ingredients Tips:

- Use different types of coffee, such as dark roast or decaf, for a variety of flavors.
- Add some smoked paprika or chili powder to the rub for a spicy kick.
- Serve the pork tenderloin with a side of roasted vegetables or mashed potatoes for a complete meal.

Per Serving: Calories: 220; Total Fat: 8g; Saturated Fat: 2g; Cholesterol: 75mg; Sodium: 75mg; Total Carbs: 11g; Fiber: 0g; Sugars: 9g; Protein: 27g

Chile Con Carne Galette

Servings: 4 | Prep Time: 20 Minutes | Cooking Time: 30 Minutes

Ingredients:

- 1 can chili beans in chili sauce
- ½ cup canned fire-roasted diced tomatoes, drained
- ½ cup grated Mexican cheese blend
- 2 teaspoons olive oil
- 225 g ground beef
- ½ cup dark beer
- ½ onion, diced
- 1 carrot, peeled and diced
- 1 celery stalk, diced
- ½ teaspoon ground cumin
- ½ teaspoon chili powder
- ¼ teaspoon salt
- 1 cup corn chips
- 3 tablespoons beef broth
- 2 teaspoons corn masa

Directions:

1. Warm the olive oil in a skillet over medium-high heat for 30 seconds. Add in ground beef, onion, carrot, and celery and cook for 5 minutes until the beef is no longer pink. Drain the fat. Mix 3 tablespoons beef broth and 2 teaspoons corn masa until smooth and then toss it in beans, chili sauce, dark beer, tomatoes, cumin, chili powder, and salt. Cook until thickened. Turn the heat off.
2. Preheat air fryer at 180°C/350°F. Spoon beef mixture into a cake pan, then top with corn chips, followed by cheese blend. Place cake pan in the frying basket and Bake for 6 minutes. Let rest for 10 minutes before serving.

Variations & Ingredients Tips:

- Use different types of beans, such as black beans or pinto beans, for a variety of flavors and textures.
- Add some diced jalapeños or hot sauce to the beef mixture for a spicy kick.
- Serve the chile con carne galette with a side of sour cream or guacamole for a creamy contrast.

Per Serving: Calories: 450; Total Fat: 22g; Saturated Fat: 8g; Cholesterol: 70mg; Sodium: 1080mg; Total Carbs: 35g; Fiber: 7g; Sugars: 5g; Protein: 26g

Egg Stuffed Pork Meatballs

Servings: 2 | Prep Time: 20 Minutes | Cooking Time: 40 Minutes

Ingredients:

- 3 soft boiled eggs, peeled
- 227 g ground pork
- 2 tsp dried tarragon
- ½ tsp hot paprika
- 2 tsp garlic powder
- Salt and pepper to taste

Directions:

1. Preheat air fryer to 175°C/350°F. Combine the pork, tarragon, hot paprika, garlic powder, salt, and pepper in a bowl and stir until all spices are evenly spread throughout the meat.
2. Divide the meat mixture into three equal portions in the mixing bowl, and shape each into balls.
3. Flatten one of the meatballs on top to make a wide, flat meat circle. Place an egg in the middle. Use your hands to mold the mixture up and around to enclose the egg. Repeat with the remaining eggs.
4. Place the stuffed balls in the air fryer. Air Fry for 18-20 minutes, shaking the basket once until the meat is crispy and golden brown. Serve.

Variations & Ingredients Tips:

- Try different spice combinations like Italian seasoning, cumin, or smoked paprika
- For a cheesy twist, add some shredded cheddar or mozzarella cheese to the meat mixture

- Serve with your favorite dipping sauce like ranch, BBQ sauce, or honey mustard

Per Serving: Calories: 435; Total Fat: 31g; Saturated Fat: 11g; Cholesterol: 394mg; Sodium: 175mg; Total Carbs: 2g; Dietary Fiber: 0g; Total Sugars: 0g; Protein: 36g

Ground Beef Calzones

Servings: 6 | Prep Time: 20 Minutes | Cooking Time: 30 Minutes

Ingredients:

- 1 refrigerated pizza dough
- 1 cup shredded mozzarella
- ½ cup chopped onion
- 2 garlic cloves, minced
- ¼ cup chopped mush-
- rooms
- 454 g ground beef
- 1 tbsp pizza seasoning
- Salt and pepper to taste
- 355 g marinara sauce
- 1 tsp flour

Directions:

1. Warm 1 tbsp of oil in a skillet over medium heat. Stir-fry onion, garlic and mushrooms for 2-3 minutes or until aromatic. Add beef, pizza seasoning, salt and pepper. Use a large spoon to break up the beef. Cook for 3 minutes or until brown. Stir in marinara sauce and set aside.
2. On a floured work surface, roll out pizza dough and cut into 6 equal-sized rectangles. On each rectangle, add ½ cup of beef and top with 1 tbsp of shredded cheese. Fold one side of the dough over the filling to the opposite side. Press the edges using the back of a fork to seal them. Preheat air fryer to 200°C/400°F. Place the first batch of calzones in the air fryer and spray with cooking oil. Bake for 10 minutes. Let cool slightly and serve warm.

Variations & Ingredients Tips:

- Use Italian sausage instead of ground beef for a spicier flavor
- Add some chopped pepperoni or ham to the filling
- Brush the calzones with garlic butter before air frying for extra richness

Per Serving: Calories: 481; Total Fat: 21g; Saturated Fat: 8g; Cholesterol: 77mg; Sodium: 912mg; Total Carbs: 44g; Dietary Fiber: 3g; Total Sugars: 6g; Protein: 30g

Friendly Bbq Baby Back Ribs

Servings: 4 | Prep Time: 10 Minutes | Cooking Time: 35 Minutes

Ingredients:

- 1 rack baby back ribs, halved
- 1 tsp onion powder
- 1 tsp garlic powder
- 1 tsp brown sugar
- 1 tsp dried oregano
- 1 tsp ancho chili powder
- 1 tsp mustard powder
- Salt and pepper to taste
- ½ cup barbecue sauce

Directions:

1. Mix the onion powder, garlic powder, brown sugar, oregano, salt, mustard, ancho chili and pepper in a small bowl. Rub the seasoning all over the meat of the ribs. Cover the ribs in plastic wrap or foil. Sit for 30 minutes.
2. Preheat air fryer to 180°C/360°F. Place all of the ribs in the air fryer. Bake for 15 minutes, then use tongs to flip the ribs. Cook for another 15 minutes. Transfer to a serving dish and drizzle with barbecue sauce. Serve and enjoy!

Variations & Ingredients Tips:

- For spicier ribs, add cayenne pepper or hot sauce to the rub
- Brush the ribs with honey or maple syrup in the last few minutes of cooking for a sticky-sweet finish
- Serve with coleslaw, baked beans and cornbread for a full barbecue feast

Per Serving: Calories: 552; Total Fat: 36g; Saturated Fat: 12g; Cholesterol: 132mg; Sodium: 819mg; Total Carbs: 22g; Dietary Fiber: 1g; Total Sugars: 18g; Protein: 36g

Flank Steak With Chimichurri Sauce

Servings: 4 | Prep Time: 20 Minutes | Cooking Time: 25 Minutes + Chilling Time

Ingredients:

- For Marinade
- 2/3 cup olive oil
- 1 tbsp Dijon mustard
- 1 orange, juiced and zested
- 1 lime, juiced and zested
- 1/3 cup tamari sauce
- 2 tbsp red wine vinegar
- 4 cloves garlic, minced
- 1 flank steak
- For Chimichurri Sauce
- 2 red jalapeños, minced
- 1 cup Italian parsley leaves
- ¼ cup cilantro leaves
- ¼ cup oregano leaves
- ¼ cup olive oil
- ½ onion, diced
- 4 cloves garlic, minced
- 2 tbsp lime juice
- 2 tsp lime zest
- 2 tbsp red wine vinegar
- ½ tsp ground cumin
- ½ tsp salt

Directions:

1. Whisk all the marinade ingredients in a large bowl. Toss in flank steak and let marinate covered for at least 1 hour.
2. In a food processor, blend parsley, cilantro, oregano, red jalapeños, olive oil, onion, garlic, lime juice, lime zest, vinegar, cumin, and salt until you reach your desired consistency. Let chill in the fridge until ready to use.
3. Preheat air fryer at 165°C/325°F. Place flank steak in the greased frying basket and Bake for 18-20 minutes until rare, turning once.
4. Let rest onto a cutting board for 5 minutes before slicing

thinly against the grain. Serve with chimichurri sauce on the side.

Variations & Ingredients Tips:

- Adjust the amount of jalapeños in the chimichurri to your desired spice level
- The chimichurri can be made a day ahead and stored in the fridge
- Flank steak can also be grilled or broiled instead of air fried

Per Serving: Calories: 697; Total Fat: 61g; Saturated Fat: 10g; Cholesterol: 68mg; Sodium: 1529mg; Total Carbs: 13g; Dietary Fiber: 3g; Total Sugars: 5g; Protein: 30g

Spicy Hoisin Bbq Pork Chops

Servings: 2 | Prep Time: 5 Minutes | Cooking Time: 12 Minutes

Ingredients:

- 3 tablespoons hoisin sauce
- ¼ cup honey
- 1 tablespoon soy sauce
- 3 tablespoons rice vinegar
- 2 tablespoons brown sugar
- 1½ teaspoons grated

- fresh ginger
- 1 to 2 teaspoons Sriracha sauce, to taste
- 2 to 3 bone-in center cut pork chops, 2.5 cm thick (about 567 g)
- chopped scallions, for garnish

Directions:

1. Combine the hoisin sauce, honey, soy sauce, rice vinegar, brown sugar, ginger, and Sriracha sauce in a small saucepan. Whisk the ingredients together and bring the mixture to a boil over medium-high heat on the stovetop. Reduce the heat and simmer the sauce until it has reduced in volume and thickened slightly – about 10 minutes.
2. Preheat the air fryer to 200°C/400°F.
3. Place the pork chops into the air fryer basket and pour half the hoisin BBQ sauce over the top. Air-fry for 6 minutes. Then, flip the chops over, pour the remaining hoisin BBQ sauce on top and air-fry for 6 more minutes, depending on the thickness of the pork chops. The internal temperature of the pork chops should be 68°C/155°F when tested with an instant read thermometer.
4. Let the pork chops rest for 5 minutes before serving. You can spoon a little of the sauce from the bottom drawer of the air fryer over the top if desired. Sprinkle with chopped scallions and serve.

Variations & Ingredients Tips:

- Use boneless pork chops or pork tenderloin for quicker cooking
- Substitute the hoisin with teriyaki sauce or Korean BBQ

sauce
- Serve with steamed rice, stir-fried veggies and extra sauce

Per Serving: Calories: 550; Total Fat: 16g; Saturated Fat: 4g; Cholesterol: 164mg; Sodium: 1377mg; Total Carbs: 61g; Dietary Fiber: 1g; Total Sugars: 55g; Protein: 47g

Italian Sausage Rolls

Servings: 4 | Prep Time: 10 Minutes | Cooking Time: 20 Minutes

Ingredients:

- 1 red bell pepper, cut into 2.5cm strips
- 4 Italian sausages (around 455g total)
- 1 zucchini, cut into 2.5cm strips
- 1/2 onion, cut into 2.5cm strips
- 1 tsp dried oregano
- 1/2 tsp garlic powder
- 5 Italian rolls

Directions:

1. Preheat air fryer to 360°F/182°C. Place all sausages in the air fryer. Bake for 10 minutes. While the sausages are cooking, season the bell pepper, zucchini and onion with oregano and garlic powder. When the time is up, flip the sausages, then add the peppers and onions. Cook for another 5 minutes or until the vegetables are soft and the sausages are cooked through. Put the sausage on Italian rolls, then top with peppers and onions. Serve.

Variations & Ingredients Tips:

- Use spicy Italian sausage for a kick of heat
- Add sauteed mushrooms or spinach to the veggie mixture
- Drizzle with marinara or pesto before serving

Per Serving: Calories: 510; Total Fat: 26g; Saturated Fat: 10g; Cholesterol: 60mg; Sodium: 1280mg; Total Carbs: 45g; Dietary Fiber: 4g; Total Sugars: 6g; Protein: 22g

Vietnamese Beef Lettuce Wraps

Servings: 4 | Prep Time: 20 Minutes | Cooking Time: 12 Minutes

Ingredients:

- 1/3 cup low-sodium soy sauce*
- 2 teaspoons fish sauce*
- 2 teaspoons brown sugar
- 1 tablespoon chili paste
- Juice of 1 lime
- 2 cloves garlic, minced
- 2 teaspoons fresh ginger, minced
- 454g beef sirloin
- Sauce
- 1/3 cup low-sodium soy sauce*
- Juice of 2 limes
- 1 tablespoon mirin wine
- 2 teaspoons chili paste
- Serving
- 1 head butter lettuce
- 1/2 cup julienned carrots
- 1/2 cup julienned cucumber
- 1/2 cup sliced radishes,

sliced into half moons · dles

2 cups cooked rice noo- · 1/3 cup chopped peanuts

Directions:

1. Combine the soy sauce, fish sauce, brown sugar, chili paste, lime juice, garlic and ginger in a bowl. Slice the beef into thin slices, then cut those slices in half. Add the beef to the marinade and marinate for 1 to 3 hours in the refrigerator. When you are ready to cook, remove the steak from the refrigerator and let it sit at room temperature for 30 minutes.
2. Preheat the air fryer to 400°F/205°C.
3. Transfer the beef and marinade to the air fryer basket. Air-fry at 400°F/205°C for 12 minutes, shaking the basket a few times during the cooking process.
4. While the beef is cooking, prepare a wrap-building station. Combine the soy sauce, lime juice, mirin wine and chili paste in a bowl and transfer to a little pouring vessel. Separate the lettuce leaves from the head of lettuce and put them in a serving bowl. Place the carrots, cucumber, radish, rice noodles and chopped peanuts all in separate serving bowls.
5. When the beef has finished cooking, transfer it to another serving bowl and invite your guests to build their wraps. To build the wraps, place some beef in a lettuce leaf and top with carrots, cucumbers, some rice noodles and chopped peanuts. Drizzle a little sauce over top, fold the lettuce around the ingredients and enjoy!

Variations & Ingredients Tips:

- Use ground beef or chicken instead of sirloin for easier prep
- Add shredded cabbage or bean sprouts to the filling
- Substitute hoison sauce for the soy sauce-lime mixture

Per Serving: Calories: 420; Total Fat: 17g; Saturated Fat: 5g; Cholesterol: 85mg; Sodium: 1280mg; Total Carbs: 35g; Dietary Fiber: 4g; Total Sugars: 10g; Protein: 32g

Mustard-crusted Rib-eye

Servings: 2 | Prep Time: 35 Minutes | Cooking Time: 9 Minutes

Ingredients:

- Two rib-eye steaks (170 g each), about 2.5 cm thick
- 1 teaspoon coarse salt
- ½ teaspoon coarse black pepper
- 2 tablespoons Dijon mustard

Directions:

1. Rub the steaks with the salt and pepper. Then spread the mustard on both sides of the steaks. Cover with foil and let the steaks sit at room temperature for 30 minutes.
2. Preheat the air fryer to 200°C/390°F.
3. Cook the steaks for 9 minutes. Check for an internal temperature of 60°C/140°F and immediately remove the steaks and let them rest for 5 minutes before slicing.

Variations & Ingredients Tips:

- Use different types of mustard, such as whole grain or spicy brown, for a variety of flavors.
- Add some minced garlic or dried herbs, such as thyme or rosemary, to the mustard coating for extra flavor.
- Serve the rib-eye steaks with a side of roasted vegetables or a baked potato for a classic steakhouse meal.

Per Serving: Calories: 390; Total Fat: 27g; Saturated Fat: 11g; Cholesterol: 115mg; Sodium: 1160mg; Total Carbs: 1g; Fiber: 0g; Sugars: 0g; Protein: 34g

Indian Fry Bread Tacos

Servings: 4 | Prep Time: 15 Minutes | Cooking Time: 20 Minutes

Ingredients:

- 1 cup all-purpose flour
- 1½ tsp salt, divided
- 1½ tsp baking powder
- ¼ cup milk
- ¼ cup warm water
- 227 g lean ground beef
- One 410g can pinto beans, drained and rinsed
- 1 tbsp taco seasoning
- ½ cup shredded cheddar cheese
- 2 cups shredded lettuce
- ¼ cup black olives, chopped
- 1 Roma tomato, diced
- 1 avocado, diced
- 1 lime

Directions:

1. In a large bowl, whisk together the flour, 1 tsp of the salt, and baking powder. Make a well in the center and add in the milk and water. Form a ball and gently knead the dough four times. Cover the bowl with a damp towel, and set aside.
2. Preheat the air fryer to 190°C/380°F.
3. In a medium bowl, mix together the ground beef, beans, and taco seasoning. Crumble the meat mixture into the air fryer basket and cook for 5 minutes; toss the meat and cook an additional 2 to 3 minutes, or until cooked fully. Place the cooked meat in a bowl for taco assembly; season with the remaining ½ tsp salt as desired.
4. On a floured surface, place the dough. Cut the dough into 4 equal parts. Using a rolling pin, roll out each piece of dough to 12.5 cm in diameter. Spray the dough with cooking spray and place in the air fryer basket, working in batches as needed. Cook for 3 minutes, flip over, spray with cooking spray, and cook for an additional 1 to 3 minutes, until golden and puffy.
5. To assemble, place the fry breads on a serving platter. Equally divide the meat and bean mixture on top of the fry bread. Divide the cheese, lettuce, olives, tomatoes, and avocado among the four tacos. Squeeze lime over the top prior to serving.

Variations & Ingredients Tips:

- Use ground turkey or shredded chicken instead of beef
- Add some sliced jalapeños or hot sauce for a spicy kick
- Offer sour cream, salsa and cilantro as additional toppings

Per Serving: Calories: 621; Total Fat: 28g; Saturated Fat: 9g; Cholesterol: 62mg; Sodium: 1472mg; Total Carbs: 64g; Dietary Fiber: 11g; Total Sugars: 3g; Protein: 30g

---

Bacon, Blue Cheese And Pear Stuffed Pork Chops

Servings: 3 | Prep Time: 15 Minutes | Cooking Time: 24 Minutes

Ingredients:

- 4 slices bacon, chopped
- 1 tablespoon butter
- ½ cup finely diced onion
- ⅓ cup chicken stock
- 1½ cups seasoned stuffing cubes
- 1 egg, beaten
- ½ teaspoon dried thyme
- ½ teaspoon salt
- ⅛ teaspoon black pepper
- 1 pear, finely diced
- ⅓ cup crumbled blue cheese
- 3 boneless center-cut pork chops (5cm thick)
- olive oil
- salt and freshly ground black pepper

Directions:

1. Preheat the air fryer to 204°C/400°F.
2. Place the bacon into the air fryer basket and air-fry for 6 minutes, stirring halfway through the cooking time. Remove the bacon and set it aside on a paper towel. Pour out the grease from the bottom of the air fryer.
3. To make the stuffing, melt the butter in a medium saucepan over medium heat on the stovetop. Add the onion and sauté for a few minutes, until it starts to soften. Add the chicken stock and simmer for 1 minute. Remove the pan from the heat and add the stuffing cubes. Stir until the stock has been absorbed. Add the egg, dried thyme, salt and freshly ground black pepper, and stir until combined. Fold in the diced pear and crumbled blue cheese.
4. Place the pork chops on a cutting board. Using the palm of your hand to hold the chop flat and steady, slice into the side of the pork chop to make a pocket in the center of the chop. Leave about an inch of chop uncut and make sure you don't cut all the way through the pork chop. Brush both sides of the pork chops with olive oil and season with salt and freshly ground black pepper. Stuff each pork chop with a third of the stuffing, packing the stuffing tightly inside the pocket.
5. Preheat the air fryer to 182°C/360°F.
6. Spray or brush the sides of the air fryer basket with oil. Place the pork chops in the air fryer basket with the open stuffed edge of the pork chop facing the outside edges of the basket.
7. Air-fry the pork chops for 18 minutes, turning the pork chops over halfway through the cooking time. When the chops are done, let them rest for 5 minutes and then transfer to a serving platter.

Variations & Ingredients Tips:

- Swap the pear for finely diced apple or dried cranberries for a different fruity flavor.
- Use gorgonzola, feta or goat cheese instead of blue cheese for a milder or tangier taste.
- Add some chopped nuts like walnuts or pecans to the stuffing for extra crunch.

Per Serving: Calories: 540; Total Fat: 30g; Saturated Fat: 12g; Cholesterol: 185mg; Sodium: 1258mg; Total Carbs: 20g; Dietary Fiber: 2g; Total Sugars: 6g; Protein: 49g

---

Tex-mex Beef Carnitas

Servings: 4 | Prep Time: 15 Minutes | Cooking Time: 30 Minutes

Ingredients:

- 567g flank steak, cut into 2.5cm strips
- 1 1/2 cups grated Colby cheese
- Salt and pepper to taste
- 2 tbsp lime juice
- 4 garlic cloves, minced
- 2 tsp chipotle powder
- 1 red bell pepper, sliced
- 1 yellow bell pepper, sliced
- 1 tbsp chili oil
- 1/2 cup salsa
- 8 corn tortillas

Directions:

1. Preheat the air fryer to 400°F/205°C. Lay the strips in a bowl and sprinkle with salt, pepper, lime juice, garlic, and chipotle powder. Toss well and let marinate. In the frying basket, combine the bell peppers and chili oil and toss.
2. Air Fry for 6 minutes or until crispy but tender. Drain the steak and discard the liquid. Lay the steak in the basket on top of the peppers and fry for 7-9 minutes more until browned. Divide the strips among tortillas and top with pepper strips, salsa, and cheese. Fold and serve.

Variations & Ingredients Tips:

- Use skirt or flank steak instead of flank steak
- Add sliced onions or jalapeños to the pepper mix
- Substitute cotija or queso fresco for the Colby cheese

Per Serving: Calories: 620; Total Fat: 29g; Saturated Fat: 12g; Cholesterol: 100mg; Sodium: 670mg; Total Carbs: 44g; Dietary Fiber: 5g; Total Sugars: 5g; Protein: 45g

---

Kentucky-style Pork Tenderloin

Servings: 2 | Prep Time: 10 Minutes | Cooking Time: 30 Minutes

Ingredients:

- 454g pork tenderloin, halved crosswise
- 1 tbsp smoked paprika
- 2 tsp ground cumin
- 1 tsp garlic powder
- 1 tsp shallot powder
- 1/4 tsp chili pepper
- Salt and pepper to taste
- 1 tsp Italian seasoning
- 2 tbsp butter, melted
- 1 tsp Worcestershire sauce

Directions:

1. Preheat air fryer to 350°F/177°C. In a shallow bowl, combine all spices. Set aside. In another bowl, whisk butter and Worcestershire sauce and brush over pork tenderloin. Sprinkle with the seasoning mix. Place pork in the lightly greased frying basket and Air Fry for 16 minutes, flipping once. Let sit onto a cutting board for 5 minutes before slicing. Serve immediately.

Variations & Ingredients Tips:

- Use smoked paprika or chipotle powder for a smoky flavor
- Add brown sugar or honey to the spice rub for a sweet-spicy glaze
- Brush tenderloin with mustard before applying rub for extra tang

Per Serving: Calories: 375; Total Fat: 16g; Saturated Fat: 7g; Cholesterol: 145mg; Sodium: 580mg; Total Carbs: 7g; Dietary Fiber: 2g; Total Sugars: 2g; Protein: 48g

Authentic Country-style Pork Ribs

Servings: 4 | Prep Time: 10 Minutes | Cooking Time: 50 Minutes

Ingredients:

- 1 teaspoon smoked paprika
- 1 teaspoon garlic powder
- 1 tablespoon honey
- 1 tablespoon BBQ sauce
- 1 onion, cut into rings
- Salt and pepper to taste
- 2 tablespoons olive oil
- 900 g country-style pork ribs

Directions:

1. Preheat air fryer at 180°C/350°F.
2. Mix all seasonings in a bowl.
3. Massage olive oil into pork ribs and sprinkle with spice mixture.
4. Place pork ribs in the greased frying basket and Air Fry for 40 minutes, flipping every 10 minutes.
5. Serve.

Variations & Ingredients Tips:

- Use different types of BBQ sauce, such as spicy or sweet, for a variety of flavors.
- Add some sliced jalapeños or red pepper flakes to the spice mixture for a spicy kick.
- Serve the pork ribs with a side of coleslaw or potato salad for a classic barbecue meal.

Per Serving: Calories: 590; Total Fat: 41g; Saturated Fat: 13g; Cholesterol: 190mg; Sodium: 330mg; Total Carbs: 8g; Fiber: 1g; Sugars: 6g; Protein: 47g

Cheesy Mushroom-stuffed Pork Loins

Servings: 3 | Prep Time: 10 Minutes | Cooking Time: 30 Minutes

Ingredients:

- 3/4 cup diced mushrooms
- 2 tsp olive oil
- 1 shallot, diced
- Salt and pepper to taste
- 3 center-cut pork loins
- 6 Gruyère cheese slices

Directions:

1. Warm the olive oil in a skillet over medium heat. Add in shallot and mushrooms and stir-fry for 3 minutes. Sprinkle with salt and pepper and cook for 1 minute.
2. Preheat air fryer to 177°C/350°F. Cut a pocket into each pork loin and set aside. Stuff an even amount of mushroom mixture into each chop pocket and top with 2 Gruyere cheese slices into each pocket. Place the pork in the lightly greased frying basket and Air Fry for 11 minutes cooked through and the cheese has melted. Let sit onto a cutting board for 5 minutes before serving.

Variations & Ingredients Tips:

- Use button or baby bella mushrooms instead of regular white mushrooms
- Add garlic, thyme or other fresh herbs to the mushroom stuffing
- Substitute Swiss, provolone or cheddar for the Gruyere cheese

Per Serving: Calories: 350; Total Fat: 20g; Saturated Fat: 8g; Cholesterol: 110mg; Sodium: 320mg; Total Carbohydrates: 4g; Dietary Fiber: 1g; Total Sugars: 1g; Protein: 37g

Crunchy Fried Pork Loin Chops

Servings: 3 | Prep Time: 15 Minutes | Cooking Time: 12 Minutes

Ingredients:

- 1 cup all-purpose flour or tapioca flour
- 1 large egg(s), well beaten
- 1½ cups seasoned Italian-style dried bread
- crumbs (gluten-free, if a concern)
- 3 boneless center-cut pork loin chops (115 to 140 g each)
- Vegetable oil spray

Directions:

1. Preheat the air fryer to 180°C/350°F.

2. Set up and fill three shallow soup plates or small pie plates on your counter: one for the flour, one for the beaten egg(s), and one for the bread crumbs.
3. Dredge a pork chop in the flour, coating both sides as well as around the edge. Gently shake off any excess, then dip the chop in the egg(s), again coating both sides and the edge. Let any excess egg slip back into the rest, then set the chop in the bread crumbs, turning it and pressing gently to coat well on both sides and the edge. Coat the pork chop all over with vegetable oil spray and set aside so you can dredge, coat, and spray the additional chop(s).
4. Set the chops in the basket with as much air space between them as possible. Air-fry undisturbed for 12 minutes, or until brown and crunchy and an instant-read meat thermometer inserted into the center of a chop registers 65°C/145°F.
5. Use kitchen tongs to transfer the chops to a wire rack. Cool for 5 minutes before serving.

Variations & Ingredients Tips:

- Use different types of seasoning, such as herbs de Provence or Cajun seasoning, for a variety of flavors.
- Add some grated Parmesan cheese or nutritional yeast to the breadcrumb mixture for a cheesy flavor.
- Serve the pork chops with a side of mashed potatoes or roasted vegetables for a complete meal.

Per Serving: Calories: 430; Total Fat: 15g; Saturated Fat: 4g; Cholesterol: 145mg; Sodium: 670mg; Total Carbs: 39g; Fiber: 2g; Sugars: 3g; Protein: 37g

Paprika Fried Beef

Servings: 4 | Prep Time: 20 Minutes | Cooking Time: 30 Minutes

Ingredients:

- Celery salt to taste
- 4 beef cube steaks
- ½ cup milk
- 1 cup flour
- 2 teaspoons paprika
- 1 egg
- 1 cup bread crumbs
- 2 tablespoons olive oil

Directions:

1. Preheat air fryer to 180°C/350°F. Place the cube steaks in a zipper sealed bag or between two sheets of cling wrap. Gently pound the steaks until they are slightly thinner. Set aside.
2. In a bowl, mix together milk, flour, paprika, celery salt, and egg until just combined. In a separate bowl, mix together the crumbs and olive oil.
3. Take the steaks and dip them into the buttermilk batter, shake off some of the excess, and return to a plate for 5 minutes. Next, dip the steaks in the bread crumbs, patting the crumbs into both sides.
4. Air Fry the steaks until the crust is crispy and brown, 12-16 minutes.
5. Serve warm.

Variations & Ingredients Tips:

- Use different types of paprika, such as smoked or hot, for a variety of flavors.
- Add some minced garlic or onion powder to the buttermilk batter for extra flavor.
- Serve the fried beef with a side of mashed potatoes or coleslaw for a classic Southern meal.

Per Serving: Calories: 500; Total Fat: 24g; Saturated Fat: 6g; Cholesterol: 140mg; Sodium: 470mg; Total Carbs: 38g; Fiber: 2g; Sugars: 2g; Protein: 35g

Oktoberfest Bratwursts

Servings: 4 | Prep Time: 5 Minutes | Cooking Time: 35 Minutes

Ingredients:

- ½ onion, cut into half-moons
- 450 g pork bratwurst links
- 2 cups beef broth
- 1 cup beer
- 2 cups drained sauerkraut
- 2 tablespoons German mustard

Directions:

1. Pierce each bratwurst with a fork twice. Place them along with beef broth, beer, 1 cup of water, and onion in a saucepan over high heat and bring to a boil. Lower the heat and simmer for 15 minutes. Drain.
2. Preheat air fryer to 200°C/400°F. Place bratwursts and onion in the frying basket and Air Fry for 3 minutes. Flip bratwursts, add the sauerkraut and cook for 3 more minutes.
3. Serve warm with mustard on the side.

Variations & Ingredients Tips:

- Use different types of beer, such as lager or ale, for a variety of flavors.
- Add some sliced bell peppers or carrots to the bratwurst mixture for extra vegetables.
- Serve the bratwursts in buns with a side of German potato salad or soft pretzels for an authentic Oktoberfest meal.

Per Serving: Calories: 450; Total Fat: 32g; Saturated Fat: 11g; Cholesterol: 80mg; Sodium: 1620mg; Total Carbs: 15g; Fiber: 3g; Sugars: 4g; Protein: 21g

Kawaii Pork Roast

Servings: 6 | Prep Time: 10 Minutes | Cooking Time: 50 Minutes

Ingredients:

- Salt and white pepper to taste

- 2 tbsp soy sauce
- 2 tbsp honey
- 1 tbsp sesame oil
- 1/4 tsp ground ginger
- 1 tsp oregano
- 2 cloves garlic, minced
- 1 boneless pork loin (around 1.4kg)

Directions:

1. Preheat air fryer at 350°F/177°C. Mix all ingredients in a bowl. Massage mixture into all sides of pork loin. Place pork loin in the greased frying basket and Roast for 40 minutes, flipping once. Let rest onto a cutting board for 5 minutes before slicing into 25cm thick slices. Serve right away.

Variations & Ingredients Tips:

- Add grated ginger or Chinese five-spice powder for more flavor
- Brush the roast with additional honey glaze halfway through cooking
- Serve sliced pork over rice or sliced on sandwiches

Per Serving: Calories: 300; Total Fat: 14g; Saturated Fat: 4g; Cholesterol: 100mg; Sodium: 500mg; Total Carbs: 8g; Dietary Fiber: 0g; Total Sugars: 6g; Protein: 35g

Rib Eye Cheesesteaks With Fried Onions

Servings: 2 | Prep Time: 15 Minutes | Cooking Time: 20 Minutes

Ingredients:

- 1 (340 g) rib eye steak
- 2 tablespoons Worcestershire sauce
- salt and freshly ground black pepper
- ½ onion, sliced
- 2 tablespoons butter, melted
- 113 g sliced Cheddar or provolone cheese
- 2 long hoagie rolls, lightly toasted

Directions:

1. Place the steak in the freezer for 30 minutes to make it easier to slice. When it is well-chilled, thinly slice the steak against the grain and transfer it to a bowl. Pour the Worcestershire sauce over the steak and season it with salt and pepper. Allow the meat to come to room temperature.
2. Preheat the air fryer to 200°C/400°F.
3. Toss the sliced onion with the butter and transfer it to the air fryer basket. Air-fry at 200°C/400°F for 12 minutes, shaking the basket a few times during the cooking process. Place the steak on top of the onions and air-fry for another 6 minutes, stirring the meat and onions together halfway through the cooking time.
4. When the air fryer has finished cooking, divide the steak and onions in half in the air fryer basket, pushing each half to one side of the air fryer basket. Place the cheese on top of each half, push the drawer back into the turned off air fryer and let it sit for 2 minutes, until the cheese has melt-

ed.
5. Transfer each half of the cheesesteak mixture into a toasted roll with the cheese side up and dig in!

Variations & Ingredients Tips:

- Add some sautéed mushrooms or bell peppers to the sandwiches
- Use Swiss cheese or spicy pepper Jack for different flavors
- Spread some garlic aioli or hot sauce on the rolls before filling

Per Serving: Calories: 835; Total Fat: 56g; Saturated Fat: 29g; Cholesterol: 175mg; Sodium: 970mg; Total Carbs: 34g; Dietary Fiber: 2g; Total Sugars: 5g; Protein: 52g

Citrus Pork Lettuce Wraps

Servings: 4 | Prep Time: 15 Minutes | Cooking Time: 35 Minutes

Ingredients:

- Salt and white pepper to taste
- 1 tablespoon cornstarch
- 1 tablespoon red wine vinegar
- 2 tablespoons orange marmalade
- 1 teaspoon pulp-free or-
- ange juice
- 2 teaspoons olive oil
- ¼ teaspoon chili pepper
- ¼ teaspoon ground ginger
- 450 g pork loin, cubed
- 8 iceberg lettuce leaves

Directions:

1. Create a slurry by whisking cornstarch and 1 tablespoon of water in a bowl. Set aside. Place a small saucepan over medium heat. Add the red wine vinegar, orange marmalade, orange juice, olive oil, chili pepper, and ginger and cook for 3 minutes, stirring continuously. Mix in the slurry and simmer for 1 more minute. Turn the heat off and let it thicken, about 3 minutes.
2. Preheat air fryer to 180°C/350°F. Sprinkle the pork with salt and white pepper. Place them in the greased frying basket and Air Fry for 8-10 minutes until cooked through and browned, turning once. Transfer pork cubes to a bowl with the sauce and toss to coat. Serve in lettuce leaves.

Variations & Ingredients Tips:

- Use different types of citrus, such as lemon or lime, for a variety of flavors.
- Add some minced garlic or shallots to the sauce for extra flavor.
- Serve the pork lettuce wraps with a side of rice or noodles for a complete meal.

Per Serving: Calories: 260; Total Fat: 9g; Saturated Fat: 2g; Cholesterol: 75mg; Sodium: 140mg; Total Carbs: 19g; Fiber: 1g; Sugars: 14g; Protein: 27g

Delicious Juicy Pork Meatballs

Servings: 4 | Prep Time: 10 Minutes | Cooking Time: 35 Minutes

Ingredients:

- ¼ cup grated cheddar cheese
- 450 g ground pork
- 1 egg
- 1 tablespoon Greek yogurt
- ½ teaspoon onion pow-der
- ¼ cup chopped parsley
- 2 tablespoons bread crumbs
- ¼ teaspoon garlic pow-der
- Salt and pepper to taste

Directions:

1. Preheat air fryer to 180°C/350°F.
2. In a bowl, combine the ground pork, egg, yogurt, onion, parsley, cheddar cheese, bread crumbs, garlic, salt, and black pepper. Form mixture into 16 meatballs.
3. Place meatballs in the lightly greased frying basket and Air Fry for 8-10 minutes, flipping once.
4. Serve.

Variations & Ingredients Tips:

- Use different types of cheese, such as mozzarella or Parmesan, for a variety of flavors.
- Add some minced jalapeño or red pepper flakes to the meatball mixture for a spicy kick.
- Serve the meatballs with a side of tomato sauce or barbecue sauce for dipping.

Per Serving: Calories: 320; Total Fat: 22g; Saturated Fat: 9g; Cholesterol: 135mg; Sodium: 280mg; Total Carbs: 5g; Fiber: 0g; Sugars: 1g; Protein: 27g

Barbecue Country-style Pork Ribs

Servings: 3 | Prep Time: 5 Minutes | Cooking Time: 30 Minutes

Ingredients:

- 3 225-g boneless coun-try-style pork ribs
- 1½ teaspoons Mild smoked paprika
- 1½ teaspoons Light brown sugar
- ¾ teaspoon Onion pow-der
- ¾ teaspoon Ground black pepper
- ¼ teaspoon Table salt
- Vegetable oil spray

Directions:

1. Preheat the air fryer to 175°C/350°F. Set the ribs in a bowl on the counter as the machine heats.
2. Mix the smoked paprika, brown sugar, onion powder, pep-per, and salt in a small bowl until well combined. Rub this mixture over all the surfaces of the country-style ribs. Gen-

erously coat the country-style ribs with vegetable oil spray.
3. Set the ribs in the basket with as much air space between them as possible. Air-fry undisturbed for 30 minutes, or until browned and sizzling and an instant-read meat ther-mometer inserted into one rib registers at least 65°C/145°F.
4. Use kitchen tongs to transfer the country-style ribs to a wire rack. Cool for 5 minutes before serving.

Variations & Ingredients Tips:

- For a spicier rub, add some cayenne pepper or chili powder.
- Brush the ribs with your favorite barbecue sauce during the last 5 minutes of cooking for extra flavor and stickiness.
- Serve with coleslaw, potato salad, or baked beans on the side.

Per Serving: Calories: 370; Total Fat: 26g; Saturated Fat: 8g; Cholesterol: 120mg; Sodium: 280mg; Total Carbohydrates: 4g; Dietary Fiber: 1g; Total Sugars: 3g; Protein: 31g

Greek Pita Pockets

Servings: 4 | Prep Time: 20 Minutes | Cooking Time: 7 Minutes

Ingredients:

- Dressing
- 1 cup plain yogurt
- 1 tbsp lemon juice
- 1 tsp dried dill weed, crushed
- 1 tsp ground oregano
- ½ tsp salt
- Meatballs
- 227 g ground lamb
- 1 tbsp diced onion
- 1 tsp dried parsley
- 1 tsp dried dill weed, crushed
- ¼ tsp oregano
- ¼ tsp coriander
- ¼ tsp ground cumin
- ¼ tsp salt
- 4 pita halves
- Suggested Toppings
- red onion, slivered
- seedless cucumber, thin-ly sliced
- crumbled Feta cheese
- sliced black olives
- chopped fresh peppers

Directions:

1. Stir dressing ingredients together and refrigerate while pre-paring lamb.
2. Combine all meatball ingredients in a large bowl and stir to distribute seasonings.
3. Shape meat mixture into 12 small meatballs, rounded or slightly flattened if you prefer.
4. Cook at 200°C/390°F for 7 minutes, until well done. Re-move and drain on paper towels.
5. To serve, pile meatballs and your choice of toppings in pita pockets and drizzle with dressing.

Variations & Ingredients Tips:

- Try using ground beef, turkey or chicken instead of lamb

- Add some chopped spinach or kale to the meatball mixture for extra veggies
- Substitute tzatziki sauce for the yogurt dressing

Per Serving: Calories: 395; Total Fat: 19g; Saturated Fat: 8g; Cholesterol: 73mg; Sodium: 788mg; Total Carbs: 32g; Dietary Fiber: 1g; Total Sugars: 4g; Protein: 25g

German-style Pork Patties

Servings: 6 | Prep Time: 10 Minutes | Cooking Time: 35 Minutes

Ingredients:

- 450g ground pork
- ¼ cup diced fresh pear
- 1 tbsp minced sage leaves
- 1 garlic clove, minced
- 2 tbsp chopped chives
- Salt and pepper to taste

Directions:

1. Preheat the air fryer to 190°C/375°F. Combine the pork, pear, sage, chives, garlic, salt, and pepper in a bowl and mix gently but thoroughly with your hands, then make 8 patties about 3 cm thick. Lay the patties in the frying basket in a single layer and Air Fry for 15-20 minutes, flipping once halfway through. Remove and drain on paper towels, then serve. Serve and enjoy!

Variations & Ingredients Tips:

- Mix in some shredded apple for extra sweetness and moisture
- Serve on pretzel buns with grainy mustard and sauerkraut
- Form the patties around cubes of Swiss cheese for a melty surprise

Per Serving: Calories: 227; Total Fat: 17g; Saturated Fat: 6g; Cholesterol: 65mg; Sodium: 80mg; Total Carbs: 2g; Dietary Fiber: 0g; Total Sugars: 1g; Protein: 16g

Fish And Seafood Recipes

Herby Prawn & Zucchini Bake

Servings: 4 | Prep Time: 10 Minutes | Cooking Time: 30 Minutes

Ingredients:

- 570g prawns, peeled and deveined
- 2 zucchini, sliced
- 2 tbsp butter, melted
- 1/2 tsp garlic salt
- 1 1/2 tsp dried oregano
- 1/8 tsp red pepper flakes
- 1/2 lemon, juiced
- 1 tbsp chopped mint
- 1 tbsp chopped dill

Directions:

1. Preheat air fryer to 175°C/350°F.
2. Combine prawns, zucchini, butter, garlic salt, oregano and pepper flakes in a bowl. Toss to coat.
3. Place prawns and zucchini in greased air fryer basket.
4. Air fry for 6-8 mins, shaking once, until zucchini is golden and prawns cooked.
5. Transfer to a plate and cover with foil.
6. Top with lemon juice, mint and dill before serving.

Variations & Ingredients Tips:

- Use different fresh herbs like parsley, basil or chives.
- Add sliced lemon or lime to the bake for extra freshness.
- Serve over rice, couscous or with crusty bread.

Per Serving: Calories: 236; Total Fat: 11g; Saturated Fat: 6g; Cholesterol: 227mg; Sodium: 965mg; Total Carbs: 9g; Dietary Fiber: 2g; Total Sugars: 4g; Protein: 26g

Classic Crab Cakes

Servings: 4 | Prep Time: 15 Minutes | Cooking Time: 10 Minutes

Ingredients:

- 280g lump crabmeat, picked over for shell and cartilage
- 6 tablespoons plain panko bread crumbs (gluten-free, if a concern)
- 6 tablespoons chopped drained jarred roasted red peppers
- 4 medium scallions, trimmed and thinly sliced
- 1/4 cup regular or low-fat mayonnaise (not fat-free; gluten-free, if a concern)
- 1/4 teaspoon dried dill
- 1/4 teaspoon dried thyme
- 1/4 teaspoon onion powder
- 1/4 teaspoon table salt
- 1/8 teaspoon celery seeds
- Up to 1/8 teaspoon cayenne
- Vegetable oil spray

Directions:

1. Preheat the air fryer to 200°C/400°F.

2. Gently mix the crabmeat, bread crumbs, red pepper, scallion, mayonnaise, dill, thyme, onion powder, salt, celery seeds, and cayenne in a bowl until well combined.
3. Use clean and dry hands to form 1/2 cup of this mixture into a tightly packed 2.5-cm-thick, 7.5- to 10-cm-wide patty. Coat the top and bottom of the patty with vegetable oil spray and set it aside. Continue making 1 more patty for a small batch, 3 more for a medium batch, or 5 more for a larger one, coating them with vegetable oil spray on both sides.
4. Set the patties in one layer in the basket and air-fry undisturbed for 10 minutes, or until lightly browned and cooked through.
5. Use a nonstick-safe spatula to transfer the crab cakes to a serving platter or plates. Wait a couple of minutes before serving.

Variations & Ingredients Tips:

- Add some Old Bay seasoning or Cajun spice to the mix.
- Form into mini crab cakes and serve as an appetizer.
- Serve with a lemon-caper aioli or spicy remoulade sauce.

Per Serving: Calories: 200; Total Fat: 12g; Saturated Fat: 2.5g; Cholesterol: 85mg; Sodium: 720mg; Total Carbs: 10g; Dietary Fiber: 1g; Total Sugars: 2g; Protein: 15g

Shrimp "scampi"

Servings: 4 | Prep Time: 5 Minutes | Cooking Time: 5 Minutes

Ingredients:

- 680g Large shrimp, peeled and deveined
- 1/4 cup Olive oil
- 2 tablespoons Minced garlic
- 1 teaspoon Dried orega-
- no
- Up to 1 teaspoon Red pepper flakes
- 1/2 teaspoon Salt
- 2 tablespoons White balsamic vinegar

Directions:

1. Preheat air fryer to 200°C/400°F.
2. Toss shrimp with oil, garlic, oregano, red pepper and salt until coated.
3. Transfer shrimp to air fryer basket, spreading in an even layer (they can overlap).
4. Air-fry 5 mins, tossing and rearranging shrimp twice so all sides are exposed.
5. Transfer shrimp to a bowl, pour vinegar over top and toss to coat.

Variations & Ingredients Tips:

- Add lemon zest or white wine to the shrimp before cooking.
- Toss cooked shrimp with parsley, red pepper flakes and butter.
- Serve over pasta, rice or with crusty bread.

Per Serving: Calories: 240; Total Fat: 13g; Saturated Fat: 2g; Cholesterol: 285mg; Sodium: 520mg; Total Carbs: 4g; Dietary Fiber: 0g; Sugars: 0g; Protein: 25g

Holiday Lobster Salad

Servings: 2 | Prep Time: 10 Minutes | Cooking Time: 20 Minutes

Ingredients:

- 2 lobster tails
- 1/4 cup mayonnaise
- 2 tsp lemon juice
- 1 stalk celery, sliced
- 2 tsp chopped chives
- 2 tsp chopped tarragon
- Salt and pepper to taste
- 2 tomato slices
- 4 cucumber slices
- 1 avocado, diced

Directions:

1. Preheat air fryer to 200°C/400°F.
2. Using kitchen shears, cut down the middle of each lobster tail on the softer side. Carefully run your finger between the lobster meat and the shell to loosen meat.
3. Place lobster tails, cut sides up, in the frying basket, and Air Fry for 8 minutes. Transfer to a large plate and let cool for 3 minutes until easy to handle, then pull lobster meat from the shell and roughly chop it.
4. Combine chopped lobster, mayonnaise, lemon juice, celery, chives, tarragon, salt, and pepper in a bowl.
5. Divide between 2 medium plates and top with tomato slices, cucumber and avocado cubes.
6. Serve immediately.

Variations & Ingredients Tips:

- Substitute lobster with crab, shrimp or crayfish.
- Add some diced red onion or fennel for crunch.
- Serve in lettuce cups, avocado halves or toasted rolls.

Per Serving: Calories: 440; Total Fat: 35g; Saturated Fat: 5g; Cholesterol: 130mg; Sodium: 620mg; Total Carbs: 12g; Dietary Fiber: 6g; Total Sugars: 3g; Protein: 24g

Spicy Fish Street Tacos With Sriracha Slaw

Servings: 2 | Prep Time: 10 Minutes | Cooking Time: 5 Minutes

Ingredients:

- Sriracha Slaw:
- 1/2 cup mayonnaise
- 2 tablespoons rice vinegar
- 1 teaspoon sugar
- 2 tablespoons sriracha chili sauce
- 5 cups shredded green cabbage
- 1/4 cup shredded carrots
- 2 scallions, chopped
- Salt and freshly ground black pepper
- Tacos:

- 1/2 cup flour
- 1 teaspoon chili powder
- 1/2 teaspoon ground cumin
- 1 teaspoon salt
- Freshly ground black pepper
- 1/2 teaspoon baking powder
- 1 egg, beaten
- 1/4 cup milk
- 1 cup breadcrumbs
- 450g mahi-mahi or snapper fillets
- 1 tablespoon canola or vegetable oil
- 6 (15cm) flour tortillas
- 1 lime, cut into wedges

Directions:

1. Make sriracha slaw by combining mayo, vinegar, sugar, sriracha in a bowl. Add cabbage, carrots, scallions and season. Refrigerate.
2. In a bowl, mix flour, chili, cumin, salt, pepper and baking powder. Add egg and milk to make a batter.
3. Cut fish into 2.5cm x 10cm strips. Dip in batter, then coat in breadcrumbs.
4. Preheat air fryer to 200°C/400°F. Spray fish with oil.
5. Air fry fish 3 mins, flip and fry 2 more mins until crispy.
6. Warm tortillas. Assemble tacos with fish, slaw and lime wedges.

Variations & Ingredients Tips:

- Use cod, tilapia or other white fish.
- Add shredded purple cabbage to the slaw.
- Serve with avocado, pico de gallo or sour cream.

Per Serving: Calories: 670; Total Fat: 26g; Saturated Fat: 4g; Cholesterol: 165mg; Sodium: 1590mg; Total Carbs: 77g; Dietary Fiber: 7g; Sugars: 11g; Protein: 35g

Herb-crusted Sole

Servings: 4 | Prep Time: 10 Minutes | Cooking Time: 20 Minutes

Ingredients:

- 1/2 lemon, juiced and zested
- 4 sole fillets
- 1/2 tsp dried thyme
- 1/2 tsp dried marjoram
- 1/2 tsp dried parsley
- Black pepper to taste
- 1 bread slice, crumbled
- 2 tsp olive oil

Directions:

1. Preheat air fryer to 160°C/320°F.
2. In a bowl, mix lemon zest, herbs, pepper, breadcrumbs and oil.
3. Arrange sole fillets skin-side down on a lined pan.
4. Pour lemon juice over fillets.
5. Press fillets into breadcrumb mixture to fully coat.
6. Air fry for 8-11 mins until breadcrumbs are crisp and golden.
7. Serve warm.

Variations & Ingredients Tips:

- Use tilapia, flounder or other thin white fish fillets.
- Add garlic powder, paprika or parmesan to the crumb mixture.
- Drizzle with melted butter or lemon butter before serving.

Per Serving: Calories: 147; Total Fat: 4g; Saturated Fat: 1g; Cholesterol: 60mg; Sodium: 193mg; Total Carbs: 8g; Dietary Fiber: 1g; Total Sugars: 1g; Protein: 19g

Horseradish Crusted Salmon

Servings: 2 | Prep Time: 10 Minutes | Cooking Time: 14 Minutes

Ingredients:

- 2 (140g) salmon fillets
- Salt and freshly ground black pepper
- 2 teaspoons Dijon mustard
- 1/2 cup panko breadcrumbs
- 2 tablespoons prepared horseradish
- 1/2 teaspoon finely chopped lemon zest
- 1 tablespoon olive oil
- 1 tablespoon chopped fresh parsley

Directions:

1. Preheat the air fryer to 180°C/360°F.
2. Season the salmon with salt and freshly ground black pepper. Then spread the Dijon mustard on the salmon, coating the entire surface.
3. Combine the breadcrumbs, horseradish, lemon zest and olive oil in a small bowl. Spread the mixture over the top of the salmon and press down lightly with your hands, adhering it to the salmon using the mustard as "glue".
4. Transfer the salmon to the air fryer basket and air-fry at 180°C/360°F for 14 minutes (depending on how thick your fillet is) or until the fish feels firm to the touch.
5. Sprinkle with the parsley.

Variations & Ingredients Tips:

- Use Dijon or whole grain mustard for a milder flavor.
- Add some grated parmesan or asiago to the breadcrumb mixture.
- Serve over a bed of sautéed spinach or roasted asparagus.

Per Serving: Calories: 400; Total Fat: 24g; Saturated Fat: 4g; Cholesterol: 85mg; Sodium: 500mg; Total Carbs: 13g; Dietary Fiber: 1g; Total Sugars: 1g; Protein: 34g

Horseradish Tuna Croquettes

Servings: 4 | Prep Time: 20 Minutes | Cooking Time: 40 Minutes

Ingredients:

- 1 can tuna in water, drained
- 1/3 cup mayonnaise
- 1 tbsp minced celery

- 1 green onion, sliced
- 2 tsp dried dill
- 1 tsp lime juice
- 1 cup bread crumbs
- 1 egg
- 1 tsp prepared horseradish

Directions:

1. Preheat air fryer to 190°C/370°F.
2. Add the tuna, mayonnaise, celery, green onion, dill, lime juice, 1/4 cup bread crumbs, egg, and horseradish in a bowl and mix to combine.
3. Mold the mixture into 12 rectangular mound shapes. Roll each croquette in a shallow dish with 3/4 cup of bread crumbs.
4. Place croquettes in the lightly greased frying basket and Air Fry for 12 minutes on all sides.
5. Serve.

Variations & Ingredients Tips:

- Use canned salmon or crab meat instead of tuna.
- Add some capers, lemon zest or Old Bay seasoning to the mix.
- Serve with a creamy dill sauce or tartar sauce.

Per Serving: Calories: 320; Total Fat: 20g; Saturated Fat: 3.5g; Cholesterol: 80mg; Sodium: 510mg; Total Carbs: 20g; Dietary Fiber: 1g; Total Sugars: 2g; Protein: 18g

Masala Fish `n´ Chips

Servings: 4 | Prep Time: 15 Minutes | Cooking Time: 30 Minutes

Ingredients:

- 2 russet potatoes, cut into strips
- 4 pollock fillets
- Salt and pepper to taste
- 1/2 tsp garam masala
- 1 egg white
- 3/4 cup bread crumbs
- 2 tbsp olive oil

Directions:

1. Preheat air fryer to 200°C/400°F.
2. Sprinkle the pollock fillets with salt, pepper, and garam masala.
3. In a shallow bowl, beat egg whites until foamy. In a separate bowl, stir together bread crumbs and 1 tablespoon olive oil until completely combined.
4. Dip the fillets into the egg white, then coat with the bread crumbs.
5. In a bowl, toss the potato strips with 1 tbsp olive oil. Place them in the frying basket and Air Fry for 10 minutes.
6. Slide-out the basket, shake the chips and place a metal holder over them. Arrange the fish fillets on the metal holder and cook for 10-12 minutes, flipping once.
7. Serve warm.

Variations & Ingredients Tips:

- Use other white fish like cod or tilapia.
- Add lemon juice or other spices to the egg wash.
- Serve with malt vinegar and tartar sauce for dipping.

Per Serving: Calories: 360; Total Fat: 13g; Saturated Fat: 2g; Cholesterol: 60mg; Sodium: 430mg; Total Carbs: 38g; Dietary Fiber: 3g; Total Sugars: 2g; Protein: 23g

Miso-rubbed Salmon Fillets

Servings: 3 | Prep Time: 10 Minutes | Cooking Time: 5 Minutes

Ingredients:

- 1/4 cup White (shiro) miso paste
- 1 1/2 tablespoons Mirin or substitute
- 2 1/2 teaspoons Unseasoned rice vinegar
- Vegetable oil spray
- 3 (170g) skin-on salmon fillets

Directions:

1. Preheat the air fryer to 200°C/400°F.
2. Mix the miso, mirin, and vinegar in a small bowl until uniform.
3. Remove basket from machine. Generously spray skin side of each fillet. Pick up with spatula and set in basket skin-side down with space between them.
4. Coat tops of fillets with miso mixture, dividing evenly.
5. Return basket to machine. Air-fry 5 minutes until lightly browned and firm.
6. Transfer fillets to plates. Cool briefly before serving.

Variations & Ingredients Tips:

- Add grated ginger or garlic to the miso rub.
- Use yellow or red miso paste for different flavors.
- Serve over steamed veggies or rice.

Per Serving: Calories: 275; Total Fat: 14g; Saturated Fat: 3g; Cholesterol: 85mg; Sodium: 630mg; Total Carbs: 4g; Fiber: 0g; Sugars: 2g; Protein: 30g

Panko-breaded Cod Fillets

Servings: 2 | Prep Time: 10 Minutes | Cooking Time: 20 Minutes

Ingredients:

- 1 lemon wedge, juiced and zested
- 1/2 cup panko bread crumbs
- Salt to taste
- 1 tbsp Dijon mustard
- 1 tbsp butter, melted
- 2 cod fillets

Directions:

1. Preheat air fryer to 175°C/350°F.

2. Combine all ingredients, except for the fish, in a bowl.
3. Press mixture evenly across tops of cod fillets.
4. Place fillets in the greased frying basket and Air Fry for 10 minutes until the cod is opaque and flakes easily with a fork.
5. Serve immediately.

Variations & Ingredients Tips:

- Use other white fish like haddock or pollock.
- Add grated parmesan or breadcrumbs to the panko coating.
- Serve with lemon wedges and tartar sauce.

Per Serving: Calories: 240; Total Fat: 7g; Saturated Fat: 3g; Cholesterol: 70mg; Sodium: 460mg; Total Carbs: 14g; Dietary Fiber: 1g; Sugars: 1g; Protein: 28g

Yummy Salmon Burgers With Salsa Rosa

Servings: 4 | Prep Time: 20 Minutes | Cooking Time: 35 Minutes + Chilling Time

Ingredients:

- 1/4 cup minced red onion
- 1/4 cup slivered onions
- 1/2 cup mayonnaise
- 2 tsp ketchup
- 1 tsp brandy
- 2 tsp orange juice
- 450g salmon fillets
- 5 tbsp panko bread crumbs
- 1 garlic clove, minced
- 1 large egg, lightly beaten
- 1 tbsp Dijon mustard
- 1 tsp fresh lemon juice
- 1 tbsp chopped parsley
- Salt to taste
- 4 buns
- 8 Boston lettuce leaves

Directions:

1. Mix the mayonnaise, ketchup, brandy, and orange juice in a bowl until blended. Set aside the resulting salsa rosa until ready to serve.
2. Cut a 115g section of salmon and place in a food processor. Pulse until it turns into a paste. Chop the remaining salmon into cubes and transfer to a bowl along with the salmon paste.
3. Add the panko, minced onion, garlic, egg, mustard, lemon juice, parsley, and salt. Toss to combine. Divide into 5 patties about 2-cm thick. Refrigerate for 30 minutes.
4. Preheat air fryer to 200°C/400°F. Place the patties in the greased frying basket. Air Fry for 12-14 minutes, flipping once until golden.
5. Serve each patty on a bun, 2 lettuce leaves, 2 tbsp of salsa rosa, and slivered onions. Enjoy!

Variations & Ingredients Tips:

- Use canned salmon instead of fresh for convenience.
- Add some diced bell peppers or jalapeños to the burger mix.

- Top with sliced avocado and crispy bacon.

Per Serving: Calories: 540; Total Fat: 34g; Saturated Fat: 6g; Cholesterol: 140mg; Sodium: 830mg; Total Carbs: 30g; Dietary Fiber: 2g; Total Sugars: 6g; Protein: 32g

Mom's Tuna Melt Toastie

Servings: 4 | Prep Time: 15 Minutes | Cooking Time: 30 Minutes

Ingredients:

- 4 white bread slices
- 60g canned tuna
- 2 tbsp mayonnaise
- 1/2 lemon, zested and juiced
- Salt and pepper to taste
- 1/2 red onion, finely sliced
- 1 red tomato, sliced
- 4 cheddar cheese slices
- 2 tbsp butter, melted

Directions:

1. Preheat air fryer to 180°C/360°F.
2. Put the butter-greased bread slices in the frying basket. Toast for 6 minutes.
3. Meanwhile, mix the tuna, lemon juice and zest, salt, pepper, and mayonnaise in a small bowl.
4. When the time is over, slide the frying basket out, flip the bread slices, and spread the tuna mixture evenly all over them.
5. Cover with tomato slices, red onion, and cheddar cheese.
6. Toast for 10 minutes or until the cheese is melted and lightly bubbling.
7. Serve and enjoy!

Variations & Ingredients Tips:

- Use whole grain or sourdough bread.
- Add sliced avocado or pickles.
- Substitute cheddar with Swiss or provolone cheese.

Per Serving: Calories: 320; Total Fat: 20g; Saturated Fat: 8g; Cholesterol: 40mg; Sodium: 550mg; Total Carbs: 21g; Fiber: 2g; Sugars: 3g; Protein: 14g

Basil Mushroom & Shrimp Spaghetti

Servings: 6 | Prep Time: 10 Minutes | Cooking Time: 20 Minutes

Ingredients:

- 225g baby Bella mushrooms, sliced
- 1/2 cup grated Parmesan
- 450g peeled shrimp, deveined
- 3 tbsp olive oil
- 1/4 tsp garlic powder
- 1/4 tsp shallot powder
- 1/4 tsp cayenne
- 450g cooked pasta spaghetti
- 5 garlic cloves, minced
- Salt and pepper to taste
- 1/2 cup dill

Directions:

1. Preheat air fryer to 190°C/380°F.
2. Toss the shrimp, 1 tbsp of olive oil, garlic powder, shallot powder and cayenne in a bowl. Put the shrimp into the frying basket and Roast for 5 minutes. Remove and set aside.
3. Warm the remaining olive oil in a large skillet over medium heat. Add the garlic and mushrooms and cook for 5 minutes.
4. Pour in the pasta, 1/2 cup of water, Parmesan, salt, pepper, and dill and stir to coat the pasta. Stir in the shrimp.
5. Remove from heat, then let the mixture rest for 5 minutes. Serve and enjoy!

Variations & Ingredients Tips:

- Use linguine, fettuccine or angel hair pasta instead of spaghetti.
- Add some halved cherry tomatoes or baby spinach leaves.
- Sprinkle with red pepper flakes for a kick of heat.

Per Serving: Calories: 390; Total Fat: 13g; Saturated Fat: 3.5g; Cholesterol: 145mg; Sodium: 440mg; Total Carbs: 43g; Dietary Fiber: 2g; Total Sugars: 2g; Protein: 28g

Baltimore Crab Cakes

Servings: 4 | Prep Time: 20 Minutes | Cooking Time: 35 Minutes

Ingredients:

- 225g lump crabmeat, shells discarded
- 2 tbsp mayonnaise
- 1/2 tsp yellow mustard
- 1/2 tsp lemon juice
- 1/2 tbsp minced shallot
- 1/4 cup bread crumbs
- 1 egg
- Salt and pepper to taste
- 4 poached eggs
- 1/2 cup bechamel sauce
- 2 tsp chopped chives
- 1 lemon, cut into wedges

Directions:

1. Preheat air fryer at 200°C/400°F.
2. Combine all ingredients, except eggs, sauce, and chives, in a bowl. Form mixture into 4 patties.
3. Place crab cakes in the greased frying basket and Air Fry for 10 minutes, flipping once.
4. Transfer them to a serving dish. Top each crab cake with 1 poached egg, drizzle with Bechamel sauce and scatter with chives and lemon wedges.
5. Serve and enjoy!

Variations & Ingredients Tips:

- Add some Old Bay seasoning or Cajun spice to the crab mixture.
- Use hollandaise sauce instead of bechamel for a classic eggs Benedict.
- Serve on toasted English muffins or brioche buns.

Per Serving: Calories: 290; Total Fat: 18g; Saturated Fat: 5g; Cholesterol: 255mg; Sodium: 620mg; Total Carbs: 10g; Dietary Fiber: 0g; Total Sugars: 2g; Protein: 22g

Saucy Shrimp

Servings: 4 | Prep Time: 15 Minutes | Cooking Time: 30 Minutes

Ingredients:

- 450g peeled shrimp, deveined
- 1/2 cup grated coconut
- 1/4 cup bread crumbs
- 1/4 cup flour
- 1/4 tsp smoked paprika
- Salt and pepper to taste
- 1 egg
- 2 tbsp maple syrup
- 1/2 tsp rice vinegar
- 1 tbsp hot sauce
- 1/8 tsp red pepper flakes
- 1/4 cup orange juice
- 1 tsp cornstarch
- 1/2 cup banana ketchup
- 1 lemon, sliced

Directions:

1. Preheat air fryer to 175°C/350°F.
2. Combine coconut, crumbs, flour, paprika, salt & pepper in a bowl.
3. In another bowl, whisk egg with 1 tsp water.
4. Dip shrimp in egg, then coat in crumb mixture.
5. Arrange shrimp in greased frying basket. Air Fry 5 mins, flip and cook 2-3 more mins.
6. Make sauce: In a pan, add syrup, ketchup, hot sauce, vinegar, pepper flakes. Make slurry with OJ and cornstarch.
7. Add slurry to pan, boil 5 mins until thick. Let sit 5 mins.
8. Serve shrimp with sauce and lemon wedges.

Variations & Ingredients Tips:

- Substitute honey or agave for maple syrup.
- Add chopped pineapple or mango to the sauce.
- Toss cooked shrimp in the sauce instead of serving on the side.

Per Serving: Calories: 290; Total Fat: 7g; Saturated Fat: 4g; Cholesterol: 170mg; Sodium: 1050mg; Total Carbs: 37g; Dietary Fiber: 2g; Sugars: 17g; Protein: 20g

Tilapia Teriyaki

Servings: 3 | Prep Time: 10 Minutes | Cooking Time: 10 Minutes

Ingredients:

- 4 tablespoons teriyaki sauce
- 1 tablespoon pineapple juice
- 450g tilapia fillets
- Cooking spray
- 170g frozen mixed peppers with onions, thawed and drained
- 2 cups cooked rice

Directions:

1. Mix the teriyaki sauce and pineapple juice together in a small bowl.
2. Split tilapia fillets down the center lengthwise.
3. Brush all sides of fish with the sauce, spray air fryer basket with nonstick cooking spray, and place fish in the basket.
4. Stir the peppers and onions into the remaining sauce and spoon over the fish. Save any leftover sauce for drizzling over the fish when serving.
5. Cook at 180°C/360°F for 10 minutes, until fish flakes easily with a fork and is done in center.
6. Divide into 3 or 4 servings and serve each with approximately 120ml/1/2 cup cooked rice.

Variations & Ingredients Tips:

- Use salmon, cod or halibut instead of tilapia.
- Add some diced pineapple or mango to the veggies.
- Sprinkle with toasted sesame seeds and sliced scallions before serving.

Per Serving: Calories: 290; Total Fat: 4g; Saturated Fat: 1g; Cholesterol: 85mg; Sodium: 810mg; Total Carbs: 34g; Dietary Fiber: 2g; Total Sugars: 9g; Protein: 30g

Mahi Mahi With Cilantro-chili Butter

Servings: 4 | Prep Time: 10 Minutes | Cooking Time: 20 Minutes

Ingredients:

- Salt and pepper to taste
- 4 mahi-mahi fillets
- 2 tbsp butter, melted
- 2 garlic cloves, minced
- 1/4 tsp chili powder
- 1/4 tsp lemon zest
- 1 tsp ginger, minced
- 1 tsp Worcestershire sauce
- 1 tbsp lemon juice
- 1 tbsp chopped cilantro

Directions:

1. Preheat air fryer to 190°C/375°F.
2. Combine butter, Worcestershire sauce, garlic, salt, lemon juice, ginger, pepper, lemon zest, and chili powder in a small bowl.
3. Place the mahi-mahi on a large plate, then spread the seasoned butter on the top of each.
4. Arrange the fish in a single layer in the parchment-lined frying basket. Bake for 6 minutes, then carefully flip the fish.
5. Bake for another 6-7 minutes until the fish is flaky and cooked through.
6. Serve immediately sprinkled with cilantro and enjoy.

Variations & Ingredients Tips:

- Use other firm white fish like cod or halibut.
- Add some cayenne pepper for extra heat.
- Serve over rice or with roasted vegetables.

Per Serving: Calories: 200; Total Fat: 8g; Saturated Fat: 4g;

Cholesterol: 120mg; Sodium: 220mg; Total Carbs: 2g; Dietary Fiber: 0g; Total Sugars: 0g; Protein: 29g

Stuffed Shrimp

Servings: 4 | Prep Time: 25 Minutes | Cooking Time: 12 Minutes Per Batch

Ingredients:

- 16 tail-on shrimp, peeled and deveined (last tail section intact)
- 3/4 cup crushed panko breadcrumbs
- Oil for misting or cooking spray
- Stuffing:
- 2 (170g) cans lump crabmeat
- 2 tablespoons chopped shallots
- 2 tablespoons chopped green onions
- 2 tablespoons chopped celery
- 2 tablespoons chopped
- green bell pepper
- 1/2 cup crushed saltine crackers
- 1 teaspoon Old Bay Seasoning
- 1 teaspoon garlic powder
- 1/4 teaspoon ground thyme
- 2 teaspoons dried parsley flakes
- 2 teaspoons fresh lemon juice
- 2 teaspoons Worcestershire sauce
- 1 egg, beaten

Directions:

1. Rinse shrimp. Remove tail section (shell) from 4 shrimp, discard, and chop the meat finely.
2. To prepare the remaining 12 shrimp, cut a deep slit down the back side so that the meat lies open flat. Do not cut all the way through.
3. Preheat air fryer to 180°C/360°F.
4. Place chopped shrimp in a large bowl with all of the stuffing ingredients and stir to combine.
5. Divide stuffing into 12 portions, about 2 tablespoons each.
6. Place one stuffing portion onto the back of each shrimp and form into a ball or oblong shape. Press firmly so that stuffing sticks together and adheres to shrimp.
7. Gently roll each stuffed shrimp in panko crumbs and mist with oil or cooking spray.
8. Place 6 shrimp in air fryer basket and cook at 180°C/360°F for 10 minutes. Mist with oil or spray and cook 2 minutes longer or until stuffing cooks through inside and is crispy outside.
9. Repeat step 8 to cook remaining shrimp.

Variations & Ingredients Tips:

- Substitute crab with cooked lobster, salmon or firm white fish.
- Add some diced jalapeño or red pepper flakes to the stuffing for heat.
- Serve with lemon wedges and a remoulade or cocktail sauce for dipping.

Per Serving: Calories: 290; Total Fat: 8g; Saturated Fat: 1.5g; Cholesterol: 230mg; Sodium: 940mg; Total Carbs: 19g; Dietary Fiber: 1g; Total Sugars: 2g; Protein: 34g

Perfect Soft-shelled Crabs

Servings: 2 | Prep Time: 10 Minutes | Cooking Time: 12 Minutes

Ingredients:

- 1/2 cup All-purpose flour
- 1 tablespoon Old Bay seasoning
- 1 Large egg, well beaten
- 1 cup (about 85g)
- Ground oyster crackers
- 2 (115g) cleaned soft-shelled crabs, about 10cm across
- Vegetable oil spray

Directions:

1. Preheat the air fryer to 190°C/375°F.
2. Set up three shallow plates: one with flour whisked with Old Bay, one for beaten egg, one for cracker crumbs.
3. Coat a crab in flour, dip in egg, coat in crumbs, pressing gently. Spray generously with oil.
4. Set crab(s) in basket with space between them, may slightly overlap.
5. Air-fry 12 minutes until crisp and golden brown. If 195°C/390°F, may be done in 10 mins.
6. Transfer crab(s) to wire rack and cool briefly before serving.

Variations & Ingredients Tips:

- Use panko breadcrumbs instead of oyster crackers.
- Substitute Cajun or blackening seasoning for Old Bay.
- Serve with lemon wedges and remoulade sauce.

Per Serving: Calories: 350; Total Fat: 10g; Saturated Fat: 3g; Cholesterol: 300mg; Sodium: 1100mg; Total Carbs: 45g; Dietary Fiber: 2g; Sugars: 2g; Protein: 23g

Shrimp Po'boy With Remoulade Sauce

Servings: 6 | Prep Time: 10 Minutes | Cooking Time: 8 Minutes

Ingredients:

- 1/2 cup all-purpose flour
- 1/2 teaspoon paprika
- 1 teaspoon garlic powder
- 1/2 teaspoon black pepper
- 1/4 teaspoon salt
- 2 eggs, whisked
- 1 1/2 cups panko bread-
- crumbs
- 450g small shrimp, peeled and deveined
- Six 15-cm French rolls
- 2 cups shredded lettuce
- 12 0.3-cm tomato slices
- 3/4 cup Remoulade Sauce

Directions:

1. Preheat air fryer to 180°C/360°F.
2. Mix flour, paprika, garlic, pepper and salt in a bowl.
3. Place eggs in a dish. Place panko in another dish.
4. Coat shrimp in flour, dip in egg, then coat in panko.
5. Spray air fryer trivet/basket with oil. Add shrimp in a single layer, spacing apart.
6. Cook 4 mins, flip and cook 4 more mins until crispy.
7. Build sandwiches with rolls, lettuce, tomato, shrimp and remoulade sauce.

Variations & Ingredients Tips:

- Use your favorite store-bought or homemade remoulade.
- Add sliced avocado or pickles to the sandwiches.
- Serve shrimp over salad greens instead of on a roll.

Per Serving: Calories: 340; Total Fat: 8g; Saturated Fat: 1g; Cholesterol: 215mg; Sodium: 790mg; Total Carbs: 45g; Dietary Fiber: 2g; Sugars: 4g; Protein: 22g

Lemon & Herb Crusted Salmon

Servings: 4 | Prep Time: 10 Minutes | Cooking Time: 20 Minutes

Ingredients:

- 1/3 cup crushed potato chips
- 4 skinless salmon fillets
- 3 tbsp honey mustard
- 1/2 tsp lemon zest
- 1/2 tsp dried thyme
- 1/2 tsp dried basil
- 1/4 cup panko bread crumbs
- 2 tbsp olive oil

Directions:

1. Preheat air fryer to 160°C/320°F.
2. Place the salmon on a work surface. Mix together mustard, lemon zest, thyme, and basil in a small bowl. Spread on top of the salmon evenly.
3. In a separate small bowl, mix together bread crumbs and potato chips before drizzling with olive oil.
4. Place the salmon in the frying basket. Bake until the salmon is cooked through and the topping is crispy and brown, about 10 minutes.
5. Serve hot and enjoy!

Variations & Ingredients Tips:

- Use Dijon or whole grain mustard instead of honey mustard.
- Add some grated parmesan or pecorino to the crust mixture.
- Serve with a side of roasted potatoes and sautéed spinach.

Per Serving: Calories: 400; Total Fat: 25g; Saturated Fat: 4.5g; Cholesterol: 85mg; Sodium: 280mg; Total Carbs: 12g; Dietary Fiber: 1g; Total Sugars: 3g; Protein: 32g

Mediterranean Salmon Burgers

Servings: 4 | Prep Time: 15 Minutes | Cooking Time: 30 Minutes

Ingredients:

- 450g salmon fillets
- 1 scallion, diced
- 4 tbsp mayonnaise
- 1 egg
- 1 tsp capers, drained
- Salt and pepper to taste
- 1/4 tsp paprika
- 1 lemon, zested
- 1 lemon, sliced
- 1 tbsp chopped dill
- 1/4 cup bread crumbs
- 4 buns, toasted
- 4 tsp whole-grain mustard
- 4 lettuce leaves
- 1 small tomato, sliced

Directions:

1. Preheat air fryer to 200°C/400°F.
2. Divide salmon in half. Cut one of the halves into chunks and transfer the chunks to the food processor. Also, add scallion, 2 tablespoons mayonnaise, egg, capers, dill, salt, pepper, paprika, and lemon zest. Pulse to puree.
3. Dice the rest of the salmon into 6mm chunks. Combine chunks and puree along with bread crumbs in a large bowl.
4. Shape the fish into 4 patties and transfer to the frying basket. Air Fry for 5 minutes, then flip the patties. Air Fry for another 5 to 7 minutes.
5. Place the patties each on a bun along with 1 teaspoon mustard, mayonnaise, lettuce, lemon slices, and a slice of tomato. Serve and enjoy.

Variations & Ingredients Tips:

- Substitute Greek yogurt for some of the mayonnaise.
- Add feta or olives to the salmon patty mixture.
- Serve on pita bread instead of buns.

Per Serving: Calories: 450, Total Fat: 23g, Saturated Fat: 4g, Cholesterol: 135mg, Sodium: 620mg, Total Carbs: 29g, Fiber: 2g, Sugars: 4g, Protein: 34g

Coconut Shrimp With Plum Sauce

Servings: 2 | Prep Time: 15 Minutes | Cooking Time: 30 Minutes

Ingredients:

- 225g raw shrimp, peeled
- 2 eggs
- 1/2 cup breadcrumbs
- 1 tsp red chili powder
- 2 tbsp dried coconut flakes
- Salt and pepper to taste
- 1/2 cup plum sauce

Directions:

1. Preheat air fryer to 180°C/350°F.
2. Whisk the eggs with salt and pepper in a bowl. Dip in the shrimp, fully submerging.

3. Combine the bread crumbs, coconut flakes, chili powder, salt, and pepper in another bowl until evenly blended.
4. Coat the shrimp in the crumb mixture and place them in the foil-lined frying basket.
5. Air Fry for 14-16 minutes. Halfway through the cooking time, shake the basket.
6. Serve with plum sauce for dipping and enjoy!

Variations & Ingredients Tips:

- Use panko breadcrumbs for an extra crispy coating.
- Add garlic powder or cajun seasoning to the breading.
- Serve with a sweet chili dipping sauce instead of plum sauce.

Per Serving: Calories: 287; Total Fat: 5g; Saturated Fat: 2g; Cholesterol: 204mg; Sodium: 915mg; Total Carbs: 35g; Dietary Fiber: 2g; Total Sugars: 10g; Protein: 26g

Quick Tuna Tacos

Servings: 4 | Prep Time: 15 Minutes | Cooking Time: 20 Minutes

Ingredients:

- 2 cups torn romaine lettuce
- 450g fresh tuna steak, cubed
- 1 tbsp grated fresh ginger
- 2 garlic cloves, minced
- 1/2 tsp toasted sesame oil
- 4 tortillas
- 1/4 cup mild salsa
- 1 red bell pepper, sliced

Directions:

1. Preheat air fryer to 200°C/390°F.
2. Combine the tuna, ginger, garlic, and sesame oil in a bowl and allow to marinate for 10 minutes.
3. Lay the marinated tuna in the fryer and Grill for 4-7 minutes.
4. Serve right away with tortillas, mild salsa, lettuce, and bell pepper for delicious tacos.

Variations & Ingredients Tips:

- Use corn or flour tortillas.
- Top with avocado, sour cream or shredded cabbage.
- Marinate the tuna longer for more flavor.

Per Serving: Calories: 270; Total Fat: 6g; Saturated Fat: 1g; Cholesterol: 55mg; Sodium: 440mg; Total Carbs: 23g; Dietary Fiber: 2g; Sugars: 2g; Protein: 31g

Flounder Fillets

Servings: 4 | Prep Time: 10 Minutes | Cooking Time: 8 Minutes

Ingredients:

- 1 egg white
- 1 tablespoon water
- 1 cup panko bread-crumbs
- 2 tablespoons extra-light
- virgin olive oil
- 4 (115g) flounder fillets
- Salt and pepper
- Oil for misting or cooking spray

Directions:

1. Preheat air fryer to 195°C/390°F.
2. Beat together egg white and water in shallow dish.
3. In another shallow dish, mix panko crumbs and oil until well combined and crumbly (best done by hand).
4. Season flounder fillets with salt and pepper to taste. Dip each fillet into egg mixture and then roll in panko crumbs, pressing in crumbs so that fish is nicely coated.
5. Spray air fryer basket with nonstick cooking spray and add fillets. Cook at 195°C/390°F for 3 minutes.
6. Spray fish fillets but do not turn. Cook 5 minutes longer or until golden brown and crispy. Using a spatula, carefully remove fish from basket and serve.

Variations & Ingredients Tips:

- Use cod, sole or tilapia instead of flounder.
- Add some grated Parmesan or lemon zest to the panko breading.
- Serve with tartar sauce, lemon wedges and steamed vegetables.

Per Serving: Calories: 230; Total Fat: 8g; Saturated Fat: 1.5g; Cholesterol: 75mg; Sodium: 300mg; Total Carbs: 13g; Dietary Fiber: 1g; Total Sugars: 1g; Protein: 25g

Fish Sticks For Grown-ups

Servings: 4 | Prep Time: 10 Minutes | Cooking Time: 6 Minutes

Ingredients:

- 450g fish fillets
- 1/2 teaspoon hot sauce
- 1 tablespoon coarse brown mustard
- 1 teaspoon Worcestershire sauce
- Salt
- Crumb Coating
- 3/4 cup panko bread-crumbs
- 1/4 cup stone-ground cornmeal
- 1/4 teaspoon salt
- Oil for misting or cooking spray

Directions:

1. Cut fish into 2.5cm wide slices across the fillet.
2. Mix hot sauce, mustard and worcestershire to make a paste. Rub on all sides of fish and season with salt.
3. Mix crumb coating ingredients and spread on wax paper.
4. Roll fish in crumb mixture to fully coat.
5. Mist all sides with oil and place in a single layer in air fryer basket.

6. Cook at 200°C/390°F for 6 minutes until fish flakes easily.

Variations & Ingredients Tips:

- Use tilapia, cod or haddock fillets.
- Add cajun seasoning or old bay to the crumb mixture.
- Serve with lemon wedges, tartar sauce or remoulade.

Per Serving: Calories: 246; Total Fat: 5g; Saturated Fat: 1g; Cholesterol: 70mg; Sodium: 441mg; Total Carbs: 19g; Dietary Fiber: 1g; Total Sugars: 1g; Protein: 30g

Shrimp, Chorizo And Fingerling Potatoes

Servings: 4 | Prep Time: 10 Minutes | Cooking Time: 16 Minutes

Ingredients:

- 1/2 red onion, chopped into 2.5cm chunks
- 8 fingerling potatoes, sliced into 2.5cm slices or halved lengthwise
- 1 teaspoon olive oil
- Salt and freshly ground black pepper
- 225g raw chorizo sausage, sliced into 2.5cm
- chunks
- 16 raw large shrimp, peeled, deveined and tails removed
- 1 lime
- 1/4 cup chopped fresh cilantro
- Chopped orange zest (optional)

Directions:

1. Preheat air fryer to 190°C/380°F.
2. Toss onion and potato chunks with olive oil, salt and pepper in a bowl.
3. Transfer veggies to air fryer basket and air-fry for 6 minutes, shaking basket periodically.
4. Add chorizo chunks and air-fry for 5 more minutes.
5. Add shrimp, season with salt and air-fry for 5 more minutes, shaking occasionally.
6. Transfer contents to a bowl and squeeze lime juice over top. Toss with cilantro, orange zest and drizzle of olive oil. Season to taste.
7. Serve with a green salad.

Variations & Ingredients Tips:

- Use cooked shrimp or a different sausage like chicken or turkey.
- Add smoked paprika or crushed red pepper for extra flavor.
- Serve in tortillas or over rice instead of a salad.

Per Serving: Calories: 400; Total Fat: 20g; Saturated Fat: 6g; Cholesterol: 170mg; Sodium: 760mg; Total Carbs: 29g; Dietary Fiber: 3g; Sugars: 2g; Protein: 26g

Fish Goujons With Tartar Sauce

Servings: 4 | Prep Time: 10 Minutes | Cooking Time: 20 Minutes

Ingredients:

- 1/4 cup flour
- Salt and pepper to taste
- 1/4 tsp smoked paprika
- 1/4 tsp dried oregano
- 1 tsp dried thyme
- 1 egg
- 4 haddock fillets
- 1 lemon, thinly sliced
- 1/2 cup tartar sauce

Directions:

1. Preheat air fryer to 200°C/400°F.
2. Combine flour, salt, pepper, paprika, thyme, and oregano in a wide bowl. Whisk egg and 1 teaspoon water in another wide bowl.
3. Slice each fillet into 4 strips. Dip the strips in the egg mixture. Then roll them in the flour mixture and coat completely.
4. Arrange the fish strips on the greased frying basket. Air Fry for 4 minutes. Flip the fish and Air Fry for another 4 to 5 minutes until crisp.
5. Serve warm with lemon slices and tartar sauce on the side and enjoy.

Variations & Ingredients Tips:

- Use cod, pollack or tilapia instead of haddock.
- Season the flour with Old Bay, lemon pepper or Cajun spice.
- Serve with malt vinegar, coleslaw or mushy peas.

Per Serving: Calories: 330; Total Fat: 17g; Saturated Fat: 2.5g; Cholesterol: 140mg; Sodium: 570mg; Total Carbs: 14g; Dietary Fiber: 1g; Total Sugars: 1g; Protein: 30g

Sweet Potato–wrapped Shrimp

Servings: 3 | Prep Time: 15 Minutes | Cooking Time: 6 Minutes

Ingredients:

- 24 Long spiralized sweet potato strands
- Olive oil spray
- ¼ tsp garlic powder
- ¼ tsp table salt
- Up to a ⅛ tsp cayenne
- 12 Large shrimp (20–25 per g), peeled and deveined

Directions:

1. Preheat the air fryer to 200°C/400°F.
2. Lay the spiralized sweet potato strands on a large swath of paper towels and straighten out the strands to long ropes. Coat them with olive oil spray, then sprinkle them with the garlic powder, salt, and cayenne.
3. Pick up 2 strands and wrap them around the center of a shrimp, with the ends tucked under what now becomes the bottom side of the shrimp. Continue wrapping the remainder of the shrimp.
4. Set the shrimp bottom side down in the basket with as much air space between them as possible. Air-fry undisturbed for 6 minutes, or until the sweet potato strands are crisp and the shrimp are pink and firm.
5. Use kitchen tongs to transfer the shrimp to a wire rack. Cool for only a minute or two before serving.

Variations & Ingredients Tips:

- Use zucchini noodles instead of sweet potato for a different flavor and texture.
- Add some paprika or chili powder to the seasoning mix for extra heat.
- Serve with a dipping sauce like sweet chili or garlic aioli.

Per Serving: Calories: 120; Total Fat: 1g; Saturated Fat: 0g; Cholesterol: 110mg; Sodium: 420mg; Total Carbohydrates: 12g; Dietary Fiber: 2g; Total Sugars: 3g; Protein: 14g

Poultry Recipes

Mexican-inspired Chicken Breasts

Servings: 4 | Prep Time: 10 Minutes | Cooking Time: 20 Minutes

Ingredients:

- 1/8 tsp crushed red pepper flakes
- 1 red pepper, deseeded and diced
- Salt to taste
- 4 chicken breasts
- 3/4 tsp garlic powder
- 1/2 tsp onion powder
- 1/2 tsp ground cumin
- 1/2 tsp ancho chile powder
- 1/2 tsp sweet paprika
- 1/2 tsp Mexican oregano
- 1 tomato, chopped
- 1/2 diced red onion
- 3 tbsp fresh lime juice
- 285g avocado, diced
- 1 tbsp chopped cilantro

Directions:

1. Preheat air fryer to 190°C/380°F.
2. Stir together salt, garlic and onion powder, cumin, ancho chili powder, paprika, Mexican oregano, and pepper flakes in a bowl.
3. Spray the chicken with cooking oil and rub with the spice mix. Air Fry the chicken for 10 minutes, flipping once until browned and fully cooked. Repeat for all of the chicken.
4. Mix the onion and lime juice in a bowl. Fold in the avocado, cilantro, red pepper, salt, and tomato and coat gently.
5. To serve, top the chicken with guacamole salsa.

Variations & Ingredients Tips:

- Use boneless, skinless chicken thighs for juicier meat.
- Add some crumbled cotija or feta cheese on top.
- Serve sliced over a bed of rice and black beans.

Per Serving: Calories: 400; Total Fat: 22g; Saturated Fat: 4g; Cholesterol: 145mg; Sodium: 420mg; Total Carbs: 10g; Dietary Fiber: 6g; Total Sugars: 3g; Protein: 44g

Simple Buttermilk Fried Chicken

Servings: 4 | Prep Time: 20 Minutes (plus At Least 1 Hour Marinating Time) | Cooking Time: 27 Minutes

Ingredients:

- 1 (1.8-kg) chicken, cut into 8 pieces
- 2 cups buttermilk
- hot sauce (optional)
- 1½ cups flour*
- 2 teaspoons paprika
- 1 teaspoon salt
- freshly ground black pepper
- 2 eggs, lightly beaten
- vegetable oil, in a spray bottle

Directions:

1. Cut the chicken into 8 pieces and submerge them in the buttermilk and hot sauce, if using. A zipper-sealable plastic bag works well for this. Let the chicken soak in the buttermilk for at least one hour or even overnight in the refrigerator.
2. Set up a dredging station. Mix the flour, paprika, salt and black pepper in a clean zipper-sealable plastic bag. Whisk the eggs and place them in a shallow dish. Remove four pieces of chicken from the buttermilk and transfer them to the bag with the flour. Shake them around to coat on all sides. Remove the chicken from the flour, shaking off any excess flour, and dip them into the beaten egg. Return the chicken to the bag of seasoned flour and shake again. Set the coated chicken aside and repeat with the remaining four pieces of chicken.
3. Preheat the air fryer to 190°C/370°F.
4. Spray the chicken on all sides with the vegetable oil and then transfer one batch to the air fryer basket. Air-fry the chicken at 190°C/370°F for 20 minutes, flipping the pieces over halfway through the cooking process, taking care not to knock off the breading. Transfer the chicken to a plate, but do not cover. Repeat with the second batch of chicken.
5. Lower the temperature on the air fryer to 170°C/340°F. Flip the chicken back over and place the first batch of chicken on top of the second batch already in the basket. Air-fry for another 7 minutes and serve warm.

Variations & Ingredients Tips:

- Use boneless, skinless chicken breasts or thighs for quicker cooking time.
- Add garlic powder, onion powder, or dried herbs to the flour mixture for extra seasoning.
- Serve with honey, hot sauce, or ranch dressing for dipping.

Per Serving: Calories: 730; Total Fat: 41g; Saturated Fat: 12g; Sodium: 980mg; Total Carbohydrates: 39g; Dietary Fiber: 2g; Total Sugars: 7g; Protein: 54g

Chicken & Fruit Biryani

Servings: 4 | Prep Time: 10 Minutes | Cooking Time: 30 Minutes

Ingredients:

- 3 chicken breasts, cubed
- 2 tsp olive oil
- 2 tbsp cornstarch
- 1 tbsp curry powder
- 1 apple, chopped
- ½ cup chicken broth
- 1/3 cup dried cranberries
- 1 cup cooked basmati rice

Directions:

1. Preheat air fryer to 190°C/380°F.
2. Combine the chicken and olive oil, then add some cornstarch and curry powder. Mix to coat, then add the apple and pour the mix in a baking pan.
3. Put the pan in the air fryer and Bake for 8 minutes, stirring once.
4. Add the chicken broth, cranberries, and 2 tbsp of water and continue baking for 10 minutes, letting the sauce thicken. The chicken should be lightly charred and cooked through.
5. Serve warm with basmati rice.

Variations & Ingredients Tips:

- Substitute chicken with cauliflower florets or paneer cheese for a vegetarian version.
- Use raisins, apricots, or figs instead of cranberries.
- Add a pinch of saffron or cardamom to the rice for extra aroma.

Per Serving: Calories: 350; Total Fat: 7g; Saturated Fat: 1g; Sodium: 250mg; Total Carbohydrates: 43g; Dietary Fiber: 4g; Total Sugars: 17g; Protein: 30g

Intense Buffalo Chicken Wings

Servings: 2 | Prep Time: 10 Minutes | Cooking Time: 40 Minutes

Ingredients:

- 8 chicken wings
- 1/2 cup melted butter
- 2 tbsp Tabasco sauce
- 1/2 tbsp lemon juice
- 1 tbsp Worcestershire
- sauce
- 2 tsp cayenne pepper
- 1 tsp garlic powder
- 1 tsp lemon zest
- Salt and pepper to taste

Directions:

1. Preheat air fryer to 175°C/350°F.
2. Place the melted butter, Tabasco, lemon juice, Worcestershire sauce, cayenne, garlic powder, lemon zest, salt, and pepper in a bowl and stir to combine.
3. Dip the chicken wings into the mixture, coating thoroughly.
4. Lay the coated chicken wings on the foil-lined frying basket in an even layer.
5. Air Fry for 16-18 minutes. Shake the basket several times during cooking until the chicken wings are crispy brown.
6. Serve.

Variations & Ingredients Tips:

- Adjust the amount of hot sauce to your spice preference.
- Use a mix of melted butter and olive oil for a healthier option.
- Serve with celery sticks and blue cheese dressing to cool the heat.

Per Serving: Calories: 600; Total Fat: 54g; Saturated Fat: 30g; Cholesterol: 210mg; Sodium: 970mg; Total Carbs: 3g; Dietary Fiber: 1g; Total Sugars: 1g; Protein: 27g

Taquitos

Servings: 12 | Prep Time: 15 Minutes | Cooking Time: 6 Minutes Per Batch

Ingredients:

- 1 teaspoon butter
- 2 tablespoons chopped green onions
- 1 cup cooked chicken, shredded
- 2 tablespoons chopped green chiles
- 56-g Pepper Jack cheese, shredded
- 4 tablespoons salsa
- 1/2 teaspoon lime juice
- 1/4 teaspoon cumin
- 1/2 teaspoon chile powder
- 1/8 teaspoon garlic powder
- 12 corn tortillas
- Oil for misting or cooking spray

Directions:

1. Melt butter and sauté green onions for 1-2 mins.
2. Remove from heat and stir in chicken, chiles, cheese, salsa, lime juice and seasonings.
3. Preheat air fryer to 200°C/390°F.
4. Warm tortillas wrapped in damp paper towels for 30-60 secs.
5. Place 1 tbsp filling in each tortilla, roll up and secure with toothpick. Mist with oil.
6. Cook taquitos in batches for 6 mins until crispy, stacking if needed.
7. Repeat for remaining taquitos.
8. Serve hot with guacamole, sour cream, salsa.

Variations & Ingredients Tips:

- Use corn or flour tortillas.
- Add black beans, corn or rice to the filling.
- Brush with egg wash before frying for a crunchier shell.

Per Serving (2 taquitos): Calories: 170; Total Fat: 7g; Saturated Fat: 3g; Cholesterol: 36mg; Sodium: 333mg; Total Carbs: 18g; Dietary Fiber: 2g; Total Sugars: 1g; Protein: 10g

Spiced Chicken Breasts

Servings: 4 | Prep Time: 5 Minutes | Cooking Time: 20 Minutes

Ingredients:

- ½ tsp dried oregano
- ½ tsp granulated garlic
- ½ tsp granulated onion
- ½ tsp chili powder
- ¼ tsp sweet paprika
- Salt and pepper to taste
- 454 grams chicken breasts, sliced

2 tbsp yellow mustard

Directions:

1. Preheat air fryer to 190°C/375°F.
2. Mix together oregano, salt, garlic, onion, chili powder, paprika, and black pepper in a small bowl.
3. Coat the chicken with mustard in a bowl. Sprinkle the seasoning mix over the chicken.
4. Place the chicken in the greased air fryer basket and Air Fry for 7-8, flipping once until cooked through.
5. Serve immediately.

Variations & Ingredients Tips:

- Use Dijon or honey mustard instead of yellow mustard for a different flavor.
- Add a squeeze of lemon or lime juice to the chicken before seasoning for brightness.
- Serve with a side of roasted vegetables or a salad for a complete meal.

Per Serving: Calories: 170; Total Fat: 3g; Saturated Fat: 0.5g; Sodium: 400mg; Total Carbohydrates: 2g; Dietary Fiber: 0g; Total Sugars: 0g; Protein: 32g

Turkey Scotch Eggs

Servings: 4 | Prep Time: 20 Minutes | Cooking Time: 30 Minutes

Ingredients:

- 680g ground turkey
- 1 tbsp ground cumin
- 1 tsp ground coriander
- 2 garlic cloves, minced
- 3 raw eggs
- 1 1/2 cups bread crumbs
- 6 hard-cooked eggs, peeled
- 1/2 cup flour

Directions:

1. Preheat air fryer to 190°C/370°F.
2. Place the ground turkey, cumin, coriander, garlic, one egg, and 1/2 cup of bread crumbs in a large bowl and mix until well incorporated.
3. Divide into 6 equal portions, then flatten each into long ovals. Set aside.
4. In a shallow bowl, beat the remaining raw eggs. In another shallow bowl, add flour. Do the same with another plate for bread crumbs.
5. Roll each cooked egg in flour, then wrap with one oval of chicken sausage until completely covered.
6. Roll again in flour, then coat in the beaten egg before rolling in bread crumbs.
7. Arrange the eggs in the greased frying basket. Air Fry for 12-14 minutes, flipping once until the sausage is cooked and the eggs are brown.
8. Serve.

Variations & Ingredients Tips:

- Use ground pork or beef instead of turkey.
- Add some cayenne pepper or smoked paprika to the meat mixture.
- Serve with a spicy mustard or Sriracha mayo dipping sauce.

Per Serving: Calories: 500; Total Fat: 26g; Saturated Fat: 7g; Cholesterol: 435mg; Sodium: 620mg; Total Carbs: 30g; Dietary Fiber: 2g; Total Sugars: 3g; Protein: 37g

Tortilla Crusted Chicken Breast

Servings: 2 | Prep Time: 10 Minutes | Cooking Time: 12 Minutes

Ingredients:

- 1/3 cup flour
- 1 teaspoon salt
- 1 1/2 teaspoons chili powder
- 1 teaspoon ground cumin
- Freshly ground black pepper
- 1 egg, beaten
- 3/4 cup coarsely crushed
- yellow corn tortilla chips
- 2 (85-115g) boneless chicken breasts
- Vegetable oil
- 1/2 cup salsa
- 1/2 cup crumbled queso fresco
- Fresh cilantro leaves
- Sour cream or guacamole (optional)

Directions:

1. Set up 3 dishes: one with flour+salt+chili powder+cumin+pepper, one with beaten egg, one with crushed tortilla chips.
2. Dredge chicken in flour, then egg, then tortilla chips, pressing to adhere.
3. Spray chicken with oil on both sides.
4. Preheat air fryer to 195°C/380°F.
5. Air fry chicken for 6 mins, flip and cook 6 more mins.
6. Serve with salsa, queso fresco, cilantro, and sour cream/guacamole if desired.

Variations & Ingredients Tips:

- Use panko breadcrumbs instead of tortilla chips.
- Add lime zest or jalapeño to the breading.
- Serve with Mexican rice and beans on the side.

Per Serving: Calories: 471; Total Fat: 19g; Saturated Fat: 4g; Cholesterol: 200mg; Sodium: 1205mg; Total Carbs: 37g; Dietary Fiber: 3g; Total Sugars: 2g; Protein: 36g

Asian-style Orange Chicken

Servings: 4 | Prep Time: 15 Minutes | Cooking Time: 25 Minutes

Ingredients:

- 454 grams chicken   breasts, cubed

- Salt and pepper to taste
- 6 tbsp cornstarch
- 1 cup orange juice
- ¼ cup orange marmalade
- ¼ cup ketchup
- ½ tsp ground ginger
- 2 tbsp soy sauce
- 1 1/3 cups edamame beans

Directions:

1. Preheat the air fryer to 190°C/375°F.
2. Sprinkle the chicken cubes with salt and pepper. Coat with 4 tbsp of cornstarch and set aside on a wire rack.
3. Mix the orange juice, marmalade, ketchup, ginger, soy sauce, and the remaining cornstarch in a cake pan, then stir in the beans.
4. Set the pan in the air fryer basket and Bake for 5-8 minutes, stirring once during cooking until the sauce is thick and bubbling. Remove from the fryer and set aside.
5. Put the chicken in the air fryer basket and fry for 10-12 minutes, shaking the basket once.
6. Stir the chicken into the sauce and beans in the pan. Return to the fryer and reheat for 2 minutes.

Variations & Ingredients Tips:

- Substitute chicken with tofu or shrimp for different protein options.
- Add sliced bell peppers, carrots, or broccoli to the sauce for extra veggies.
- Serve over steamed rice, quinoa, or noodles for a complete meal.

Per Serving: Calories: 400; Total Fat: 6g; Saturated Fat: 1g; Sodium: 830mg; Total Carbohydrates: 52g; Dietary Fiber: 5g; Total Sugars: 25g; Protein: 34g

Super-simple Herby Turkey

Servings: 4 | Prep Time: 10 Minutes | Cooking Time: 35 Minutes

Ingredients:

- 2 turkey tenderloins
- 2 tbsp olive oil
- Salt and pepper to taste
- 2 tbsp minced rosemary
- 1 tbsp minced thyme
- 1 tbsp minced sage

Directions:

1. Preheat the air fryer to 175°C/350°F.
2. Brush the tenderloins with olive oil and sprinkle with salt and pepper.
3. Mix rosemary, thyme, and sage, then rub the seasoning onto the meat.
4. Put the tenderloins in the frying basket and Bake for 22-27 minutes, flipping once until cooked through.
5. Lay the turkey on a serving plate, cover with foil, and let stand for 5 minutes. Slice before serving.

Variations & Ingredients Tips:

- Use a turkey breast instead of tenderloins, adjusting cooking time.
- Add garlic powder or onion powder to the herb mix.
- Brush with melted butter before cooking for extra richness.

Per Serving: Calories: 196; Total Fat: 7g; Saturated Fat: 1g; Cholesterol: 91mg; Sodium: 90mg; Total Carbs: 1g; Dietary Fiber: 0g; Total Sugars: 0g; Protein: 31g

Chicken Parmigiana

Servings: 2 | Prep Time: 10 Minutes | Cooking Time: 35 Minutes

Ingredients:

- 2 chicken breasts
- 1 cup breadcrumbs
- 2 eggs, beaten
- Salt and pepper to taste
- 1 tbsp dried basil
- 1 cup passata
- 2 provolone cheese slices
- 1 tbsp Parmesan cheese

Directions:

1. Preheat air fryer to 175°C/350°F.
2. Mix breadcrumbs, basil, salt and pepper in a bowl.
3. Coat chicken in breadcrumb mixture, then egg, then breadcrumbs again.
4. Arrange coated chicken in greased air fryer basket.
5. Air fry for 20 mins, flipping halfway through.
6. Pour half the passata into a baking pan. Place cooked chicken over it.
7. Top with remaining passata, provolone and parmesan.
8. Bake for 5 more mins until cheese is melted.
9. Serve hot.

Variations & Ingredients Tips:

- Use marinara sauce instead of passata.
- Add garlic powder or Italian herbs to the breadcrumb mixture.
- Serve over pasta or with roasted vegetables.

Per Serving: Calories: 574; Total Fat: 18g; Saturated Fat: 8g; Cholesterol: 256mg; Sodium: 947mg; Total Carbs: 51g; Dietary Fiber: 3g; Total Sugars: 6g; Protein: 51g

Indian Chicken Tandoori

Servings: 2 | Prep Time: 10 Minutes (plus Marinating Time) | Cooking Time: 35 Minutes

Ingredients:

- 2 chicken breasts, cubed
- 1/2 cup hung curd
- 1 tsp turmeric powder
- 1 tsp red chili powder
- 1 tsp chaat masala powder
- Pinch of salt

Directions:

1. Preheat air fryer to 175°C/350°F.
2. Mix the hung curd, turmeric, red chili powder, chaat masala powder, and salt in a mixing bowl. Stir until the mixture is free of lumps.
3. Coat the chicken with the mixture, cover, and refrigerate for 30 minutes to marinate.
4. Place the marinated chicken chunks in a baking pan and drizzle with the remaining marinade.
5. Bake for 25 minutes until the chicken is juicy and spiced.
6. Serve warm.

Variations & Ingredients Tips:

- Use Greek yogurt instead of hung curd for a tangy flavor.
- Add minced garlic and ginger to the marinade for extra zing.
- Garnish with fresh cilantro and squeeze of lime juice.

Per Serving: Calories: 220; Total Fat: 3g; Saturated Fat: 1g; Cholesterol: 105mg; Sodium: 370mg; Total Carbs: 4g; Dietary Fiber: 1g; Total Sugars: 2g; Protein: 41g

Enchilada Chicken Quesadillas

Servings: 4 | Prep Time: 15 Minutes | Cooking Time: 35 Minutes

Ingredients:

- 2 cups cooked chicken breasts, shredded
- 1 can (120g) diced green chilies, including juice
- 2 cups grated Mexican cheese blend
- 3/4 cup sour cream
- 2 tsp chili powder
- 1 tsp cumin
- 1 tbsp chipotle sauce
- 1 tsp dried onion flakes
- 1/2 tsp salt
- 3 tbsp butter, melted
- 8 flour tortillas

Directions:

1. In a small bowl, whisk the sour cream, chipotle sauce and chili powder. Let chill in the fridge until ready to use.
2. Preheat air fryer at 175°C/350°F.
3. Mix the chicken, green chilies, cumin, and salt in a bowl. Set aside.
4. Brush on one side of a tortilla lightly with melted butter. Layer with 1/4 cup of chicken, onion flakes and 1/4 cup of Mexican cheese. Top with a second tortilla and lightly brush with butter on top. Repeat with the remaining ingredients.
5. Place quesadillas, butter side down, in the frying basket and Bake for 3 minutes.
6. Cut them into 6 sections and serve with cream sauce on the side.

Variations & Ingredients Tips:

- Use corn tortillas for a gluten-free option.

- Add sautéed bell peppers and onions to the chicken mixture.
- Top with sliced avocado, salsa and cilantro.

Per Serving: Calories: 660; Total Fat: 41g; Saturated Fat: 22g; Cholesterol: 160mg; Sodium: 1230mg; Total Carbs: 35g; Dietary Fiber: 2g; Total Sugars: 3g; Protein: 37g

Rich Turkey Burgers

Servings: 4 | Prep Time: 10 Minutes | Cooking Time: 30 Minutes

Ingredients:

- 2 tbsp finely grated Emmental
- 1/3 cup minced onions
- ¼ cup grated carrots
- 2 garlic cloves, minced
- 2 tsp olive oil
- 1 tsp dried marjoram
- 1 egg
- 454 grams ground turkey

Directions:

1. Preheat air fryer to 200°C/400°F.
2. Mix the onions, carrots, garlic, olive oil, marjoram, Emmental, and egg in a bowl, then add the ground turkey. Use your hands to mix the ingredients together.
3. Form the mixture into 4 patties. Set them in the air fryer and Air Fry for 18-20 minutes, flipping once until cooked through and golden.
4. Serve.

Variations & Ingredients Tips:

- Use ground chicken, pork, or beef instead of turkey for different meats.
- Add chopped spinach, kale, or mushrooms to the patty mixture for extra veggies.
- Serve on a bun with lettuce, tomato, and your favorite condiments.

Per Serving: Calories: 290; Total Fat: 18g; Saturated Fat: 5g; Sodium: 170mg; Total Carbohydrates: 4g; Dietary Fiber: 1g; Total Sugars: 1g; Protein: 29g

Mexican Chicken Roll-ups

Servings: 4 | Prep Time: 15 Minutes | Cooking Time: 35 Minutes

Ingredients:

- 1/2 red bell pepper, cut into strips
- 1/2 green bell pepper, cut into strips
- 2 chicken breasts
- 1/2 lime, juiced
- 2 tbsp taco seasoning
- 1 spring onion, thinly sliced

Directions:

1. Preheat air fryer to 200°C/400°F.
2. Cut the chicken into cutlets by slicing the chicken breast in half horizontally in order to have 4 thin cutlets. Drizzle with lime juice and season with taco seasoning.
3. Divide the red pepper, green pepper, and spring onion equally between the 4 cutlets. Roll up the cutlets. Secure with toothpicks.
4. Place the chicken roll-ups in the air fryer and lightly spray with cooking oil. Bake for 12 minutes, turning once.
5. Serve warm.

Variations & Ingredients Tips:

- Add some shredded cheddar or pepper jack cheese inside the rolls.
- Serve with salsa, guacamole or sour cream for dipping.
- Use large lettuce leaves instead of bell peppers for a low-carb option.

Per Serving: Calories: 150; Total Fat: 3g; Saturated Fat: 0.5g; Cholesterol: 75mg; Sodium: 400mg; Total Carbs: 4g; Dietary Fiber: 1g; Total Sugars: 2g; Protein: 27g

Classic Chicken Cobb Salad

Servings:4 | Prep Time: 20 Minutes | Cooking Time: 30 Minutes

Ingredients:

- 113 grams cooked bacon, crumbled
- 2 chicken breasts, cubed
- 1 tbsp sesame oil
- Salt and pepper to taste
- 4 cups torn romaine lettuce
- 2 tbsp olive oil
- 1 tbsp white wine vinegar
- 2 hard-boiled eggs, sliced
- 2 tomatoes, diced
- 6 radishes, finely sliced
- ¼ cup blue cheese crumbles
- ¼ cup diced red onions
- 1 avocado, diced

Directions:

1. Preheat air fryer to 180°C/350°F.
2. Combine chicken cubes, sesame oil, salt, and black pepper in a bowl.
3. Place chicken cubes in the air fryer basket and Air Fry for 9 minutes, flipping once. Reserve.
4. In a bowl, combine the lettuce, olive oil, and vinegar. Divide between 4 bowls.
5. Add in the cooked chicken, hard-boiled egg slices, bacon, tomato cubes, radishes, blue cheese, onion, and avocado cubes.
6. Serve.

Variations & Ingredients Tips:

- Substitute chicken with shrimp, steak, or tofu for different protein options.
- Add sliced cucumbers, bell peppers, or carrots for extra veggies.
- Use a different dressing like ranch, honey mustard, or balsamic vinaigrette.

Per Serving: Calories: 520; Total Fat: 40g; Saturated Fat: 11g; Sodium: 620mg; Total Carbohydrates: 13g; Dietary Fiber: 7g; Total Sugars: 4g; Protein: 32g

Spinach & Turkey Meatballs

Servings: 4 | Prep Time: 10 Minutes | Cooking Time: 45 Minutes

Ingredients:

- 1/4 cup grated Parmesan cheese
- 2 scallions, chopped
- 1 garlic clove, minced
- 1 egg, beaten
- 1 cup baby spinach
- 1/4 cup bread crumbs
- 1 tsp dried oregano
- Salt and pepper to taste
- 565g ground turkey

Directions:

1. Preheat the air fryer to 205°C/400°F and preheat the oven to 120°C/250°F.
2. Combine the scallions, garlic, egg, baby spinach, breadcrumbs, Parmesan, oregano, salt, and pepper in a bowl and mix well.
3. Add the turkey and mix, then form into 3.8cm meatballs.
4. Add as many meatballs as will fit in a single layer in the frying basket and Air Fry for 10-15 minutes, shaking once around minute 7.
5. Put the cooked meatballs on a tray in the oven and cover with foil to keep warm. Repeat with the remaining balls.

Variations & Ingredients Tips:

- Add breadcrumbs if mixture seems too wet to form balls.
- Use ground chicken or beef instead of turkey.
- Serve meatballs with marinara sauce for dipping.

Per Serving (6 meatballs): Calories: 268; Total Fat: 13g; Saturated Fat: 4g; Cholesterol: 136mg; Sodium: 455mg; Total Carbs: 10g; Dietary Fiber: 1g; Total Sugars: 1g; Protein: 28g

Buttered Chicken Thighs

Servings: 4 | Prep Time: 10 Minutes | Cooking Time: 30 Minutes

Ingredients:

- 4 bone-in chicken thighs, skinless
- 2 tbsp butter, melted
- 1 tsp garlic powder
- 1 tsp lemon zest
- Salt and pepper to taste
- 1 lemon, sliced

Directions:

1. Preheat air fryer to 190°C/380°F.
2. Stir the chicken thighs in the butter, lemon zest, garlic powder, and salt.
3. Divide the chicken thighs between 4 pieces of foil and sprinkle with black pepper, and then top with slices of lemon.
4. Bake in the air fryer for 20-22 minutes until golden.
5. Serve.

Variations & Ingredients Tips:

- Use boneless, skinless chicken thighs for quicker cooking time.
- Add dried herbs like thyme, rosemary, or oregano to the butter mixture.
- Squeeze lemon juice over the chicken after cooking for extra brightness.

Per Serving: Calories: 280; Total Fat: 19g; Saturated Fat: 8g; Sodium: 230mg; Total Carbohydrates: 1g; Dietary Fiber: 0g; Total Sugars: 0g; Protein: 26g

Fiery Chicken Meatballs

Servings: 4 | Prep Time: 15 Minutes | Cooking Time: 20 Minutes + Chilling Time

Ingredients:

- 2 jalapeños, seeded and diced
- 2 tbsp shredded Cheddar cheese
- 1 tsp Quick Pickled Jalapeños
- 2 tbsp white wine vinegar
- 1/2 tsp granulated sugar
- Salt and pepper to taste
- 1 tbsp ricotta cheese
- 340g ground chicken
- 1/4 tsp smoked paprika
- 1 tsp garlic powder
- 1 cup bread crumbs
- 1/4 tsp salt

Directions:

1. Combine the jalapeños, white wine vinegar, sugar, black pepper, and salt in a bowl. Let sit the jalapeño mixture in the fridge for 15 minutes.
2. In a bowl, combine ricotta cheese, cheddar cheese, and 1 tsp of the jalapeños. Form mixture into 8 balls.
3. Mix the ground chicken, smoked paprika, garlic powder, and salt in a bowl. Form mixture into 8 meatballs. Form a hole in the chicken meatballs, press a cheese ball into the hole and form chicken around the cheese ball, sealing the cheese ball in meatballs.
4. Preheat air fryer at 175°C/350°F. Mix the breadcrumbs and salt in a bowl. Roll stuffed meatballs in the mixture. Place the meatballs in the greased frying basket. Air Fry for 10 minutes, turning once.
5. Serve immediately.

Variations & Ingredients Tips:

- Use diced pickled jalapeños instead of fresh for a milder

heat.
- Mix some chopped cilantro or parsley into the chicken.
- Serve with ranch or blue cheese dressing for dipping.

Per Serving: Calories: 270; Total Fat: 13g; Saturated Fat: 5g; Cholesterol: 115mg; Sodium: 610mg; Total Carbs: 14g; Dietary Fiber: 1g; Total Sugars: 2g; Protein: 24g

Christmas Chicken & Roasted Grape Salad

Servings: 4 | Prep Time: 20 Minutes | Cooking Time: 40 Minutes

Ingredients:

- 3 chicken breasts, pat-dried
- 1 tsp paprika
- Salt and pepper to taste
- 2 cups seedless red grapes
- ½ cup mayonnaise
- ½ cup plain yogurt
- 2 tbsp honey mustard
- 2 tbsp fresh lemon juice
- 1 cup chopped celery
- 2 scallions, chopped
- 2 tbsp walnuts, chopped

Directions:

1. Preheat the air fryer to 190°C/370°F.
2. Sprinkle the chicken breasts with paprika, salt, and pepper. Transfer to the greased air fryer basket and Air Fry for 16-19 minutes, flipping once. Remove and set on a cutting board.
3. Put the grapes in the fryer and spray with cooking oil. Fry for 4 minutes or until the grapes are hot and tender.
4. Mix the mayonnaise, yogurt, honey mustard, and lemon juice in a bowl and whisk.
5. Cube the chicken and add to the dressing along with the grapes, walnuts, celery, and scallions. Toss gently and serve.

Variations & Ingredients Tips:

- Use turkey, duck, or Cornish game hen instead of chicken for a festive twist.
- Substitute grapes with dried cranberries, cherries, or figs.
- Add chopped apples, pears, or persimmons for a fruity crunch.

Per Serving: Calories: 450; Total Fat: 29g; Saturated Fat: 5g; Sodium: 400mg; Total Carbohydrates: 20g; Dietary Fiber: 2g; Total Sugars: 15g; Protein: 32g

Sandwiches And Burgers Recipes

Provolone Stuffed Meatballs

Servings: 4 | Prep Time: 20 Minutes | Cooking Time: 12 Minutes

Ingredients:

- 1 tablespoon olive oil
- 1 small onion, very finely chopped
- 1 to 2 cloves garlic, minced
- 340 grams ground beef
- 340 grams ground pork
- ¾ cup breadcrumbs
- ¼ cup grated Parmesan cheese
- ¼ cup finely chopped
- fresh parsley (or 1 tablespoon dried parsley)
- ½ teaspoon dried oregano
- 1½ teaspoons salt
- freshly ground black pepper
- 2 eggs, lightly beaten
- 140 grams sharp or aged provolone cheese, cut into 2.5-cm cubes

Directions:

1. Preheat a skillet over medium-high heat. Add the oil and cook the onion and garlic until tender, but not browned.
2. Transfer the onion and garlic to a large bowl and add the beef, pork, breadcrumbs, Parmesan cheese, parsley, oregano, salt, pepper and eggs. Mix well until all the ingredients are combined. Divide the mixture into 12 evenly sized balls. Make one meatball at a time, by pressing a hole in the meatball mixture with your finger and pushing a piece of provolone cheese into the hole. Mold the meat back into a ball, enclosing the cheese.
3. Preheat the air fryer to 190°C/380°F.
4. Working in two batches, transfer six of the meatballs to the air fryer basket and air-fry for 12 minutes, shaking the basket and turning the meatballs a couple of times during the cooking process. Repeat with the remaining six meatballs. You can pop the first batch of meatballs into the air fryer for the last two minutes of cooking to re-heat them. Serve warm.

Variations & Ingredients Tips:

- Substitute beef and pork with ground turkey or chicken for a leaner meatball option.
- Use mozzarella or fontina cheese instead of provolone for a milder flavor.
- Serve meatballs with marinara sauce, in sub rolls, or over pasta for a complete meal.

Per Serving (3 meatballs): Calories: 520; Cholesterol: 180mg; Total Fat: 36g; Saturated Fat: 15g; Sodium: 1160mg; Total Carbohydrates: 18g; Dietary Fiber: 1g; Total Sugars: 2g; Protein: 35g

Sausage And Pepper Heros

Servings: 3 | Prep Time: 10 Minutes | Cooking Time: 11 Minutes

Ingredients:

- 3 links (about 255 grams total) Sweet Italian sausages (gluten-free, if a concern)
- 1½ Medium red or green bell pepper(s), stemmed, cored, and cut into 1.25-cm-wide strips
- 1 medium Yellow or white onion(s), peeled, halved, and sliced into
- thin half-moons
- 3 Long soft rolls, such as hero, hoagie, or Italian sub rolls (gluten-free, if a concern), split open lengthwise
- For garnishing Balsamic vinegar
- For garnishing Fresh basil leaves

Directions:

1. Preheat the air fryer to 200°C/400°F.
2. When the machine is at temperature, set the sausage links in the basket in one layer and air-fry undisturbed for 5 minutes.
3. Add the pepper strips and onions. Continue air-frying, tossing and rearranging everything about once every minute, for 5 minutes, or until the sausages are browned and an instant-read meat thermometer inserted into one of the links registers 70°C/160°F.
4. Use a nonstick-safe spatula and kitchen tongs to transfer the sausages and vegetables to a cutting board. Set the rolls cut side down in the basket in one layer (working in batches as necessary) and air-fry undisturbed for 1 minute, to toast the rolls a bit and warm them up. Set 1 sausage with some pepper strips and onions in each warm roll, sprinkle balsamic vinegar over the sandwich fillings, and garnish with basil leaves.

Variations & Ingredients Tips:

- Use hot Italian sausage or chorizo for a spicier sandwich.
- Add sliced mushrooms or zucchini to the pepper and onion mixture for extra veggies.
- Top with shredded mozzarella or provolone cheese for a cheesy twist.

Per Serving (1 sandwich): Calories: 560; Cholesterol: 60mg; Total Fat: 36g; Saturated Fat: 12g; Sodium: 1420mg; Total Carbohydrates: 39g; Dietary Fiber: 3g; Total Sugars: 7g; Protein: 24g

Dijon Thyme Burgers

Servings: 3 | Prep Time: 15 Minutes | Cooking Time: 18 Minutes

Ingredients:

- 450 grams lean ground beef
- ⅓ cup panko bread-crumbs
- ¼ cup finely chopped onion
- 3 tablespoons Dijon mustard
- 1 tablespoon chopped fresh thyme
- 4 teaspoons Worcester-shire sauce
- 1 teaspoon salt
- freshly ground black pepper
- Topping (optional):
- 2 tablespoons Dijon mustard
- 1 tablespoon dark brown sugar
- 1 teaspoon Worcester-shire sauce
- 115 grams sliced Swiss cheese, optional

Directions:

1. Combine all the burger ingredients together in a large bowl and mix well. Divide the meat into 4 equal portions and then form the burgers, being careful not to over-handle the meat. One good way to do this is to throw the meat back and forth from one hand to another, packing the meat each time you catch it. Flatten the balls into patties, making an indentation in the center of each patty with your thumb (this will help it stay flat as it cooks) and flattening the sides of the burgers so that they will fit nicely into the air fryer basket.
2. Preheat the air fryer to 190°C/370°F.
3. If you don't have room for all four burgers, air-fry two or three burgers at a time for 8 minutes. Flip the burgers over and air-fry for another 6 minutes.
4. While the burgers are cooking combine the Dijon mustard, dark brown sugar, and Worcestershire sauce in a small bowl and mix well. This optional topping to the burgers really adds a boost of flavor at the end. Spread the Dijon topping evenly on each burger. If you cooked the burgers in batches, return the first batch to the cooker at this time – it's ok to place the fourth burger on top of the others in the center of the basket. Air-fry the burgers for another 3 minutes.
5. Finally, if desired, top each burger with a slice of Swiss cheese. Lower the air fryer temperature to 165°C/330°F and air-fry for another minute to melt the cheese. Serve the burgers on toasted brioche buns, dressed the way you like them.

Variations & Ingredients Tips:

- Use ground turkey or chicken for a leaner burger option.
- Add minced garlic or finely chopped herbs like parsley or chives for extra flavor.
- Substitute panko breadcrumbs with regular breadcrumbs or oats for a different texture.

Per Serving (1 burger with cheese): Calories: 500; Cholesterol: 120mg; Total Fat: 27g; Saturated Fat: 11g; Sodium: 1180mg; Total Carbohydrates: 21g; Dietary Fiber: 1g; Total Sugars: 5g; Protein: 41g

White Bean Veggie Burgers

Servings: 3 | Prep Time: 15 Minutes | Cooking Time: 13 Minutes

Ingredients:

- 320 grams Drained and rinsed canned white beans
- 3 tablespoons Rolled oats (not quick-cooking or steel-cut; gluten-free, if a concern)
- 3 tablespoons Chopped walnuts
- 2 teaspoons Olive oil
- 2 teaspoons Lemon juice
- 1½ teaspoons Dijon mustard (gluten-free, if a concern)
- ¾ teaspoon Dried sage leaves
- ¼ teaspoon Table salt
- Olive oil spray
- 3 Whole-wheat buns or gluten-free whole-grain buns (if a concern), split open

Directions:

1. Preheat the air fryer to 200°C/400°F.
2. Place the beans, oats, walnuts, oil, lemon juice, mustard, sage, and salt in a food processor. Cover and process to make a coarse paste that will hold its shape, about like wet sugar-cookie dough, stopping the machine to scrape down the inside of the canister at least once.
3. Scrape down and remove the blade. With clean and wet hands, form the bean paste into two 10-cm patties for the small batch, three 10-cm patties for the medium, or four 10-cm patties for the large batch. Generously coat the patties on both sides with olive oil spray.
4. Set them in the basket with some space between them and air-fry undisturbed for 12 minutes, or until lightly brown and crisp at the edges. The tops of the burgers will feel firm to the touch.
5. Use a nonstick-safe spatula, and perhaps a flatware fork for balance, to transfer the burgers to a cutting board. Set the buns cut side down in the basket in one layer (working in batches as necessary) and air-fry undisturbed for 1 minute, to toast a bit and warm up. Serve the burgers warm in the buns.

Variations & Ingredients Tips:

- Use black beans, chickpeas, or lentils instead of white beans for a different flavor and color.
- Add grated carrots, zucchini, or beets to the burger mixture for extra nutrition and texture.
- Serve with your favorite burger toppings like lettuce, tomato, onion, and pickles.

Per Serving (1 burger): Calories: 350; Cholesterol: 0mg; Total Fat: 13g; Saturated Fat: 1g; Sodium: 520mg; Total Carbohydrates: 48g; Dietary Fiber: 9g; Total Sugars: 4g; Protein:

14g

Chicken Saltimbocca Sandwiches

Servings: 3 | Prep Time: 10 Minutes | Cooking Time: 11 Minutes

Ingredients:

- 3 140to 170-gram boneless skinless chicken breasts
- 6 Thin prosciutto slices
- 6 Provolone cheese slices
- 3 Long soft rolls, such

as hero, hoagie, or Italian sub rolls (gluten-free, if a concern), split open lengthwise
- 3 tablespoons Pesto, purchased or homemade (see the headnote)

Directions:

1. Preheat the air fryer to 200°C/400°F.
2. Wrap each chicken breast with 2 prosciutto slices, spiraling the prosciutto around the breast and overlapping the slices a bit to cover the breast. The prosciutto will stick to the chicken more readily than bacon does.
3. When the machine is at temperature, set the wrapped chicken breasts in the basket and air-fry undisturbed for 10 minutes, or until the prosciutto is frizzled and the chicken is cooked through.
4. Overlap 2 cheese slices on each breast. Air-fry undisturbed for 1 minute, or until melted. Take the basket out of the machine.
5. Smear the insides of the rolls with the pesto, then use kitchen tongs to put a wrapped and cheesy chicken breast in each roll.

Variations & Ingredients Tips:

- Use fresh mozzarella instead of provolone for a creamier texture.
- Add sliced tomatoes or roasted red peppers for extra flavor and nutrition.
- Substitute prosciutto with ham or bacon if desired.

Per Serving: Calories: 630; Cholesterol: 125mg; Total Fat: 32g; Saturated Fat: 11g; Sodium: 1580mg; Total Carbohydrates: 38g; Dietary Fiber: 2g; Total Sugars: 4g; Protein: 48g

Eggplant Parmesan Subs

Servings: 2 | Prep Time: 10 Minutes | Cooking Time: 13 Minutes

Ingredients:

- 4 Peeled eggplant slices (about 1.25 cm thick and 7.5 cm in diameter)
- Olive oil spray

- 2 tablespoons plus 2 teaspoons Jarred pizza sauce, any variety except creamy

- ¼ cup (about 20 grams) Finely grated Parmesan cheese
- 2 Small, long soft rolls,

such as hero, hoagie, or Italian sub rolls (gluten-free, if a concern), split open lengthwise

Directions:

1. Preheat the air fryer to 175°C/350°F.
2. When the machine is at temperature, coat both sides of the eggplant slices with olive oil spray. Set them in the basket in one layer and air-fry undisturbed for 10 minutes, until lightly browned and softened.
3. Increase the machine's temperature to 190°C/375°F (or 185°C/370°F, if that's the closest setting—unless the machine is already at 180°C/360°F, in which case leave it alone). Top each eggplant slice with 2 teaspoons pizza sauce, then 1 tablespoon of cheese. Air-fry undisturbed for 2 minutes, or until the cheese has melted.
4. Use a nonstick-safe spatula, and perhaps a flatware fork for balance, to transfer the eggplant slices cheese side up to a cutting board. Set the roll(s) cut side down in the basket in one layer (working in batches as necessary) and air-fry undisturbed for 1 minute, to toast the rolls a bit and warm them up. Set 2 eggplant slices in each warm roll.

Variations & Ingredients Tips:

- Use zucchini slices instead of eggplant for a different vegetable option.
- Add a slice of fresh mozzarella on top of the Parmesan for extra cheesiness.
- Sprinkle some dried herbs like oregano or basil on the eggplant before cooking for extra flavor.

Per Serving (1 sandwich): Calories: 280; Cholesterol: 10mg; Total Fat: 9g; Saturated Fat: 3g; Sodium: 840mg; Total Carbohydrates: 40g; Dietary Fiber: 5g; Total Sugars: 8g; Protein: 11g

Best-ever Roast Beef Sandwiches

Servings: 6 | Prep Time: 10 Minutes | Cooking Time: 30-50 Minutes

Ingredients:

- 2½ teaspoons Olive oil
- 1½ teaspoons Dried oregano
- 1½ teaspoons Dried thyme
- 1½ teaspoons Onion powder
- 1½ teaspoons Table salt
- 1½ teaspoons Ground black pepper
- 1 kg Beef eye of round
- 6 Round soft rolls, such

as Kaiser rolls or hamburger buns (gluten-free, if a concern), split open lengthwise
- ¾ cup Regular, low-fat, or fat-free mayonnaise (gluten-free, if a concern)
- 6 Romaine lettuce leaves, rinsed
- 6 Round tomato slices (0.5 cm thick)

Directions:

1. Preheat the air fryer to 180°C/350°F .
2. Mix the oil, oregano, thyme, onion powder, salt, and pepper in a small bowl. Spread this mixture all over the eye of round.
3. When the machine is at temperature, set the beef in the basket and air-fry for 30 to 50 minutes (the range depends on the size of the cut), turning the meat twice, until an instant-read meat thermometer inserted into the thickest piece of the meat registers 55°C/130°F for rare, 60°C/140°F for medium, or 65°C/150°F for well-done.
4. Use kitchen tongs to transfer the beef to a cutting board. Cool for 10 minutes. If serving now, carve into 3-mm-thick slices. Spread each roll with 2 tablespoons mayonnaise and divide the beef slices between the rolls. Top with a lettuce leaf and a tomato slice and serve. Or set the beef in a container, cover, and refrigerate for up to 3 days to make cold roast beef sandwiches anytime.

Variations & Ingredients Tips:

- Experiment with different herbs and spices in the rub, such as garlic powder, paprika, or rosemary.
- Add sliced red onions or pickles for extra flavor and crunch.
- Use leftover roast beef for cold sandwiches or salads.

Per Serving: Calories: 560; Cholesterol: 115mg; Total Fat: 27g; Saturated Fat: 6g; Sodium: 980mg; Total Carbohydrates: 32g; Dietary Fiber: 2g; Total Sugars: 4g; Protein: 47g

Mexican Cheeseburgers

Servings: 4 | Prep Time: 20 Minutes | Cooking Time: 22 Minutes

Ingredients:

- 570 grams ground beef
- ¼ cup finely chopped onion
- ½ cup crushed yellow corn tortilla chips
- 1 (35-gram) packet taco seasoning
- ¼ cup canned diced green chilies
- 1 egg, lightly beaten
- 115 grams pepper jack cheese, grated
- 4 (30-cm) flour tortillas
- shredded lettuce, sour cream, guacamole, salsa (for topping)

Directions:

1. Combine the ground beef, minced onion, crushed tortilla chips, taco seasoning, green chilies, and egg in a large bowl. Mix thoroughly until combined – your hands are good tools for this. Divide the meat into four equal portions and shape each portion into an oval-shaped burger.
2. Preheat the air fryer to 190°C/370°F.
3. Air-fry the burgers for 18 minutes, turning them over halfway through the cooking time. Divide the cheese between the burgers, lower fryer to 170°C/340°F and air-fry for an additional 4 minutes to melt the cheese. (This will give you a burger that is medium-well. If you prefer your cheeseburger medium-rare, shorten the cooking time to about 15 minutes and then add the cheese and proceed with the recipe.)
4. While the burgers are cooking, warm the tortillas wrapped in aluminum foil in a 175°C/350°F oven, or in a skillet with a little oil over medium-high heat for a couple of minutes. Keep the tortillas warm until the burgers are ready.
5. To assemble the burgers, spread sour cream over three quarters of the tortillas and top each with some shredded lettuce and salsa. Place the Mexican cheeseburgers on the lettuce and top with guacamole. Fold the tortillas around the burger, starting with the bottom and then folding the sides in over the top. (A little sour cream can help hold the seam of the tortilla together.) Serve immediately.

Variations & Ingredients Tips:

- Use ground turkey or chicken for a leaner burger option.
- Substitute pepper jack cheese with Monterey Jack or cheddar cheese if preferred.
- Add sliced jalapeños or hot sauce to the burger mixture for extra heat.

Per Serving (1 burger): Calories: 780; Cholesterol: 165mg; Total Fat: 44g; Saturated Fat: 18g; Sodium: 1480mg; Total Carbohydrates: 51g; Dietary Fiber: 4g; Total Sugars: 4g; Protein: 46g

Chili Cheese Dogs

Servings: 3 | Prep Time: 10 Minutes | Cooking Time: 12 Minutes

Ingredients:

- 340 grams Lean ground beef
- 1½ tablespoons Chile powder
- 240 grams plus 2 tablespoons Jarred sofrito
- 3 Hot dogs (gluten-free, if a concern)
- 3 Hot dog buns (gluten-free, if a concern), split open lengthwise
- 3 tablespoons Finely chopped scallion
- 60 grams Shredded Cheddar cheese

Directions:

1. Crumble the ground beef into a medium or large saucepan set over medium heat. Brown well, stirring often to break up the clumps. Add the chile powder and cook for 30 seconds, stirring the whole time. Stir in the sofrito and bring to a simmer. Reduce the heat to low and simmer, stirring occasionally, for 5 minutes. Keep warm.
2. Preheat the air fryer to 200°C/400°F.
3. When the machine is at temperature, put the hot dogs in the basket and air-fry undisturbed for 10 minutes, or until the hot dogs are bubbling and blistered, even a little crisp.
4. Use kitchen tongs to put the hot dogs in the buns. Top each

with about 120 grams of the ground beef mixture, 1 tablespoon of the minced scallion, and 20 grams of the cheese. (The scallion should go under the cheese so it superheats and wilts a bit.) Set the filled hot dog buns in the basket and air-fry undisturbed for 2 minutes, or until the cheese has melted.

5. Remove the basket from the machine. Cool the chili cheese dogs in the basket for 5 minutes before serving.

Variations & Ingredients Tips:

● Use turkey or veggie hot dogs for a healthier option.
● Substitute cheddar cheese with your favorite melty cheese, such as pepper jack or Swiss.
● Add diced onions or jalapeños to the chili for extra flavor and heat.

Per Serving: Calories: 580; Cholesterol: 110mg; Total Fat: 32g; Saturated Fat: 13g; Sodium: 1420mg; Total Carbohydrates: 36g; Dietary Fiber: 5g; Total Sugars: 6g; Protein: 38g

Reuben Sandwiches

Servings: 2 | Prep Time: 10 Minutes | Cooking Time: 11 Minutes

Ingredients:

● 225 grams Sliced deli corned beef
● 4 teaspoons Regular or low-fat mayonnaise (not fat-free)
● 4 Rye bread slices
● 2 tablespoons plus 2 teaspoons Russian dressing
● ½ cup Purchased sauerkraut, squeezed by the handful over the sink to get rid of excess moisture
● 55 grams (2 to 4 slices) Swiss cheese slices (optional)

Directions:

1. Set the corned beef in the basket, slip the basket into the machine, and heat the air fryer to 200°C/400°F. Air-fry undisturbed for 3 minutes from the time the basket is put in the machine, just to warm up the meat.

2. Use kitchen tongs to transfer the corned beef to a cutting board. Spread 1 teaspoon mayonnaise on one side of each slice of rye bread, rubbing the mayonnaise into the bread with a small flatware knife.

3. Place the bread slices mayonnaise side down on a cutting board. Spread the Russian dressing over the "dry" side of each slice. For one sandwich, top one slice of bread with the corned beef, sauerkraut, and cheese (if using). For two sandwiches, top two slices of bread each with half of the corned beef, sauerkraut, and cheese (if using). Close the sandwiches with the remaining bread, setting it mayonnaise side up on top.

4. Set the sandwich(es) in the basket and air-fry undisturbed for 8 minutes, or until browned and crunchy.

5. Use a nonstick-safe spatula, and perhaps a flatware fork for balance, to transfer the sandwich(es) to a cutting board.

Cool for 2 or 3 minutes before slicing in half and serving.

Variations & Ingredients Tips:

● Substitute corned beef with pastrami for a classic New York deli taste.
● Use Thousand Island dressing instead of Russian dressing for a tangy, sweet flavor.
● Add sliced dill pickles or mustard to the sandwich for extra zing.

Per Serving (1 sandwich): Calories: 520; Cholesterol: 75mg; Total Fat: 30g; Saturated Fat: 9g; Sodium: 2020mg; Total Carbohydrates: 36g; Dietary Fiber: 4g; Total Sugars: 6g; Protein: 29g

Chicken Spiedies

Servings: 3 | Prep Time: 15 Minutes (plus Marinating Time) | Cooking Time: 12 Minutes

Ingredients:

● 570 grams Boneless skinless chicken thighs, trimmed of any fat blobs and cut into 5-cm pieces
● 3 tablespoons Red wine vinegar
● 2 tablespoons Olive oil
● 2 tablespoons Minced fresh mint leaves
● 2 tablespoons Minced fresh parsley leaves
● 2 teaspoons Minced fresh dill fronds
● ¾ teaspoon Fennel seeds
● ¾ teaspoon Table salt
● Up to a ¼ teaspoon Red pepper flakes
● 3 Long soft rolls, such as hero, hoagie, or Italian sub rolls (gluten-free, if a concern), split open lengthwise
● 4½ tablespoons Regular or low-fat mayonnaise (not fat-free; gluten-free, if a concern)
● 1½ tablespoons Distilled white vinegar
● 1½ teaspoons Ground black pepper

Directions:

1. Mix the chicken, vinegar, oil, mint, parsley, dill, fennel seeds, salt, and red pepper flakes in a zip-closed plastic bag. Seal, gently massage the marinade ingredients into the meat, and refrigerate for at least 2 hours or up to 6 hours. (Longer than that and the meat can turn rubbery.)

2. Set the plastic bag out on the counter (to make the contents a little less frigid). Preheat the air fryer to 200°C/400°F.

3. When the machine is at temperature, use kitchen tongs to set the chicken thighs in the basket (discard any remaining marinade) and air-fry undisturbed for 6 minutes. Turn the thighs over and continue air-frying undisturbed for 6 minutes more, until well browned, cooked through, and even a little crunchy.

4. Dump the contents of the basket onto a wire rack and cool for 2 or 3 minutes. Divide the chicken evenly between the rolls. Whisk the mayonnaise, vinegar, and black pepper in a small bowl until smooth. Drizzle this sauce over the chicken pieces in the rolls.

Variations & Ingredients Tips:

- Use chicken breast instead of thighs for a leaner option.
- Substitute the herbs with your favorite combination, such as basil, oregano, or thyme.
- Add sliced onions or pickled vegetables for extra crunch and tanginess.

Per Serving: Calories: 710; Cholesterol: 200mg; Total Fat: 44g; Saturated Fat: 8g; Sodium: 1240mg; Total Carbohydrates: 37g; Dietary Fiber: 2g; Total Sugars: 4g; Protein: 45g

Inside-out Cheeseburgers

Servings: 3 | Prep Time: 15 Minutes | Cooking Time: 9-11 Minutes

Ingredients:

- 510 grams 90% lean ground beef
- ¾ teaspoon Dried oregano
- ¾ teaspoon Table salt
- ¾ teaspoon Ground black pepper
- ¼ teaspoon Garlic powder
- 6 tablespoons (about 45 grams) Shredded Cheddar, Swiss, or other semi-firm cheese, or a purchased blend of shredded cheeses
- 3 Hamburger buns (gluten-free, if a concern), split open

Directions:

1. Preheat the air fryer to 190°C/375°F.
2. Gently mix the ground beef, oregano, salt, pepper, and garlic powder in a bowl until well combined without turning the mixture to mush. Form it into two 15-cm patties for the small batch, three for the medium, or four for the large.
3. Place 2 tablespoons of the shredded cheese in the center of each patty. With clean hands, fold the sides of the patty up to cover the cheese, then pick it up and roll it gently into a ball to seal the cheese inside. Gently press it back into a 12.5-cm burger without letting any cheese squish out. Continue filling and preparing more burgers, as needed.
4. Place the burgers in the basket in one layer and air-fry undisturbed for 8 minutes for medium or 10 minutes for well-done. (An instant-read meat thermometer won't work for these burgers because it will hit the mostly melted cheese inside and offer a hotter temperature than the surrounding meat.)
5. Use a nonstick-safe spatula, and perhaps a flatware fork for balance, to transfer the burgers to a cutting board. Set the buns cut side down in the basket in one layer (working in batches as necessary) and air-fry undisturbed for 1 minute, to toast a bit and warm up. Cool the burgers a few minutes more, then serve them warm in the buns.

Variations & Ingredients Tips:

- Mix different types of cheese like cheddar, mozzarella, and blue cheese for a flavorful combination.

- Add finely chopped bacon or caramelized onions to the cheese stuffing for extra richness.
- Serve with your favorite burger toppings like lettuce, tomato, onion, and pickles.

Per Serving (1 burger): Calories: 480; Cholesterol: 125mg; Total Fat: 27g; Saturated Fat: 11g; Sodium: 720mg; Total Carbohydrates: 22g; Dietary Fiber: 1g; Total Sugars: 3g; Protein: 38g

Crunchy Falafel Balls

Servings: 8 | Prep Time: 15 Minutes | Cooking Time: 16 Minutes

Ingredients:

- 600 grams Drained and rinsed canned chickpeas
- 60 grams Olive oil
- 3 tablespoons All-purpose flour
- 1½ teaspoons Dried oregano
- 1½ teaspoons Dried sage leaves
- 1½ teaspoons Dried thyme
- ¾ teaspoon Table salt
- Olive oil spray

Directions:

1. Preheat the air fryer to 200°C/400°F.
2. Place the chickpeas, olive oil, flour, oregano, sage, thyme, and salt in a food processor. Cover and process into a paste, stopping the machine at least once to scrape down the inside of the canister.
3. Scrape down and remove the blade. Using clean, wet hands, form 2 tablespoons of the paste into a ball, then continue making 9 more balls for a small batch, 15 more for a medium one, and 19 more for a large batch. Generously coat the balls in olive oil spray.
4. Set the balls in the basket in one layer with a little space between them and air-fry undisturbed for 16 minutes, or until well browned and crisp.
5. Dump the contents of the basket onto a wire rack. Cool for 5 minutes before serving.

Variations & Ingredients Tips:

- Add minced garlic, onion, or herbs like parsley or cilantro for extra flavor.
- Serve with tahini sauce, hummus, or tzatziki for dipping.
- Make a falafel sandwich by stuffing pita bread with falafel balls, lettuce, tomato, and sauce.

Per Serving (2 falafel balls): Calories: 170; Cholesterol: 0mg; Total Fat: 9g; Saturated Fat: 1g; Sodium: 230mg; Total Carbohydrates: 18g; Dietary Fiber: 4g; Total Sugars: 2g; Protein: 5g

Black Bean Veggie Burgers

Servings: 3 | Prep Time: 15 Minutes | Cooking

Ingredients:

- 1 cup Drained and rinsed canned black beans
- ⅓ cup Pecan pieces
- ⅓ cup Rolled oats (not quick-cooking or steel-cut; gluten-free, if a concern)
- 2 tablespoons (or 1 small egg) Pasteurized egg substitute, such as Egg Beaters (gluten-free, if a concern)
- 2 teaspoons Red ketchup-like chili sauce, such as Heinz
- ¼ teaspoon Ground cumin
- ¼ teaspoon Dried oregano
- ¼ teaspoon Table salt
- ¼ teaspoon Ground black pepper
- Olive oil
- Olive oil spray

Directions:

1. Preheat the air fryer to 200°C/400°F.
2. Put the beans, pecans, oats, egg substitute or egg, chili sauce, cumin, oregano, salt, and pepper in a food processor. Cover and process to a coarse paste that will hold its shape like sugar-cookie dough, adding olive oil in 1-teaspoon increments to get the mixture to blend smoothly. The amount of olive oil is actually dependent on the internal moisture content of the beans and the oats. Figure on about 1 tablespoon (three 1-teaspoon additions) for the smaller batch, with proportional increases for the other batches. A little too much olive oil can't hurt, but a dry paste will fall apart as it cooks and a far-too-wet paste will stick to the basket.
3. Scrape down and remove the blade. Using clean, wet hands, form the paste into two 10 cm patties for the small batch, three 10 cm patties for the medium, or four 10 cm patties for the large batch, setting them one by one on a cutting board. Generously coat both sides of the patties with olive oil spray.
4. Set them in the basket in one layer. Air-fry undisturbed for 10 minutes, or until lightly browned and crisp at the edges.
5. Use a nonstick-safe spatula, and perhaps a flatware fork for balance, to transfer the burgers to a wire rack. Cool for 5 minutes before serving.

Variations & Ingredients Tips:

- Add finely chopped vegetables like bell peppers, onions, or carrots for extra flavor and nutrition.
- Experiment with different spices and herbs, such as smoked paprika, garlic powder, or cilantro.
- For a gluten-free version, ensure all ingredients are certified gluten-free.

Per Serving: Calories: 280; Cholesterol: 0mg; Total Fat: 15g; Saturated Fat: 2g; Sodium: 420mg; Total Carbohydrates: 28g; Dietary Fiber: 8g; Total Sugars: 2g; Protein: 10g

Salmon Burgers

Servings: 3 | Prep Time: 15 Minutes | Cooking

Ingredients:

- 510 grams Skinless salmon fillet, preferably fattier Atlantic salmon
- 1½ tablespoons Minced chives or the green part of a scallion
- ½ cup Plain panko bread crumbs (gluten-free, if a concern)
- 1½ teaspoons Dijon mustard (gluten-free, if a concern)
- 1½ teaspoons Drained and rinsed capers, minced
- 1½ teaspoons Lemon juice
- ¼ teaspoon Table salt
- ¼ teaspoon Ground black pepper
- Vegetable oil spray

Directions:

1. Preheat the air fryer to 190°C/375°F.
2. Cut the salmon into pieces that will fit in a food processor. Cover and pulse until coarsely chopped. Add the chives and pulse to combine, until the fish is ground but not a paste. Scrape down and remove the blade. Scrape the salmon mixture into a bowl. Add the bread crumbs, mustard, capers, lemon juice, salt, and pepper. Stir gently until well combined.
3. Use clean and dry hands to form the mixture into two 12.5-cm patties for a small batch, three 12.5-cm patties for a medium batch, or four 12.5-cm patties for a large one.
4. Coat both sides of each patty with vegetable oil spray. Set them in the basket in one layer and air-fry undisturbed for 8 minutes, or until browned and an instant-read meat thermometer inserted into the center of a burger registers 65°C/145°F.
5. Use a nonstick-safe spatula, and perhaps a flatware fork for balance, to transfer the burgers to a wire rack. Cool for 2 or 3 minutes before serving.

Variations & Ingredients Tips:

- Substitute salmon with canned or leftover cooked salmon for convenience.
- Add finely chopped red bell pepper or celery to the burger mixture for extra crunch and flavor.
- Serve on toasted buns with lettuce, tomato, and a dollop of tartar sauce or remoulade.

Per Serving (1 burger): Calories: 320; Cholesterol: 95mg; Total Fat: 16g; Saturated Fat: 3g; Sodium: 440mg; Total Carbohydrates: 15g; Dietary Fiber: 1g; Total Sugars: 1g; Protein: 31g

Philly Cheesesteak Sandwiches

Servings: 3 | Prep Time: 10 Minutes | Cooking Time: 9 Minutes

Ingredients:

- 340 grams Shaved beef
- 1 tablespoon Worcestershire sauce (gluten-free, if a concern)
- ¼ teaspoon Garlic powder
- ¼ teaspoon Mild paprika
- 6 tablespoons (45 grams) Frozen bell pepper strips (do not thaw)
- 2 slices, broken into rings Very thin yellow or white medium onion slice(s)
- 170 grams (6 to 8 slices) Provolone cheese slices
- 3 Long soft rolls such as hero, hoagie, or Italian sub rolls, or hot dog buns (gluten-free, if a concern), split open lengthwise

Directions:

1. Preheat the air fryer to 200°C/400°F.
2. When the machine is at temperature, spread the shaved beef in the basket, leaving a 1.25-cm perimeter around the meat for good air flow. Sprinkle the meat with the Worcestershire sauce, paprika, and garlic powder. Spread the peppers and onions on top of the meat.
3. Air-fry undisturbed for 6 minutes, or until cooked through. Set the cheese on top of the meat. Continue air-frying undisturbed for 3 minutes, or until the cheese has melted.
4. Use kitchen tongs to divide the meat and cheese layers in the basket between the rolls or buns. Serve hot.

Variations & Ingredients Tips:

- Use thinly sliced ribeye or sirloin steak instead of shaved beef for a more traditional texture.
- Add sliced mushrooms to the pepper and onion mixture for extra flavor and nutrition.
- Substitute provolone with American cheese or Cheez Whiz for a classic Philly taste.

Per Serving: Calories: 620; Cholesterol: 135mg; Total Fat: 32g; Saturated Fat: 15g; Sodium: 1320mg; Total Carbohydrates: 38g; Dietary Fiber: 2g; Total Sugars: 5g; Protein: 48g

Asian Glazed Meatballs

Servings: 4 | Prep Time: 15 Minutes | Cooking Time: 10 Minutes

Ingredients:

- 1 large shallot, finely chopped
- 2 cloves garlic, minced
- 1 tablespoon grated fresh ginger
- 2 teaspoons fresh thyme, finely chopped
- 1½ cups brown mushrooms, very finely chopped (a food processor works well here)
- 2 tablespoons soy sauce
- freshly ground black pepper
- ½ kg ground beef
- ¼ kg ground pork
- 3 egg yolks
- 1 cup Thai sweet chili sauce (spring roll sauce)
- ¼ cup toasted sesame seeds
- 2 scallions, sliced

Directions:

1. Combine the shallot, garlic, ginger, thyme, mushrooms, soy sauce, freshly ground black pepper, ground beef and pork, and egg yolks in a bowl and mix the ingredients together. Gently shape the mixture into 24 balls, about the size of a golf ball.
2. Preheat the air fryer to 190°C/380°F.
3. Working in batches, air-fry the meatballs for 8 minutes, turning the meatballs over halfway through the cooking time. Drizzle some of the Thai sweet chili sauce on top of each meatball and return the basket to the air fryer, air-frying for another 2 minutes. Reserve the remaining Thai sweet chili sauce for serving.
4. As soon as the meatballs are done, sprinkle with toasted sesame seeds and transfer them to a serving platter. Scatter the scallions around and serve warm.

Variations & Ingredients Tips:

- Use a food processor to finely chop the mushrooms for better texture in the meatballs.
- Work in batches when air frying the meatballs to ensure even cooking and browning.
- Drizzle the Thai sweet chili sauce over the meatballs towards the end of cooking for a nice glaze.

Per Serving: Calories: 550; Cholesterol: 205mg; Total Fat: 32g; Saturated Fat: 11g; Sodium: 1300mg; Total Carbohydrates: 36g; Dietary Fiber: 2g; Total Sugars: 23g; Protein: 29g

Lamb Burgers

Servings: 3 | Prep Time: 15 Minutes | Cooking Time: 17 Minutes

Ingredients:

- 510 grams Ground lamb
- 3 tablespoons Crumbled feta
- 1 teaspoon Minced garlic
- 1 teaspoon Tomato paste
- ¾ teaspoon Ground coriander
- ¾ teaspoon Ground dried ginger
- Up to ⅛ teaspoon Cayenne
- Up to a ⅛ teaspoon Table salt (optional)
- 3 Kaiser rolls or hamburger buns (gluten-free, if a concern), split open

Directions:

1. Preheat the air fryer to 190°C/375°F.
2. Gently mix the ground lamb, feta, garlic, tomato paste, coriander, ginger, cayenne, and salt (if using) in a bowl until well combined, trying to keep the bits of cheese intact. Form this mixture into two 15-cm patties for the small batch, three 12.5-cm patties for the medium, or four 12.5-cm patties for the large.
3. Set the patties in the basket in one layer and air-fry undisturbed for 16 minutes, or until an instant-read meat thermometer inserted into one burger registers 70°C/160°F. (The cheese is not an issue with the temperature probe in

this recipe as it was for the Inside-Out Cheeseburgers, because the feta is so well mixed into the ground meat.)

4. Use a nonstick-safe spatula, and perhaps a flatware fork for balance, to transfer the burgers to a cutting board. Set the buns cut side down in the basket in one layer (working in batches as necessary) and air-fry undisturbed for 1 minute, to toast a bit and warm up. Serve the burgers warm in the buns.

Variations & Ingredients Tips:

- Substitute feta with goat cheese or crumbled blue cheese for a different flavor profile.
- Add finely chopped mint or parsley to the lamb mixture for a fresh, herbal taste.
- Serve with tzatziki sauce, sliced cucumbers, and red onions for a Greek-inspired burger.

Per Serving (1 burger): Calories: 560; Cholesterol: 140mg; Total Fat: 34g; Saturated Fat: 15g; Sodium: 580mg; Total Carbohydrates: 25g; Dietary Fiber: 1g; Total Sugars: 3g; Protein: 38g

Chicken Apple Brie Melt

Servings: 3 | Prep Time: 10 Minutes | Cooking Time: 13 Minutes

Ingredients:

- 3 140 to 170-gram boneless skinless chicken breasts
- Vegetable oil spray
- 1½ teaspoons Dried herbes de Provence
- 85 grams Brie, rind removed, thinly sliced
- 6 Thin cored apple slices
- 3 French rolls (gluten-free, if a concern)
- 2 tablespoons Dijon mustard (gluten-free, if a concern)

Directions:

1. Preheat the air fryer to 190°C/375°F .
2. Lightly coat all sides of the chicken breasts with vegetable oil spray. Sprinkle the breasts evenly with the herbes de Provence.
3. When the machine is at temperature, set the breasts in the basket and air-fry undisturbed for 10 minutes.
4. Top the chicken breasts with the apple slices, then the cheese. Air-fry undisturbed for 2 minutes, or until the cheese is melty and bubbling.
5. Use a nonstick-safe spatula and kitchen tongs, for balance, to transfer the breasts to a cutting board. Set the rolls in the basket and air-fry for 1 minute to warm through. (Putting them in the machine without splitting them keeps the insides very soft while the outside gets a little crunchy.)
6. Transfer the rolls to the cutting board. Split them open lengthwise, then spread 1 teaspoon mustard on each cut side. Set a prepared chicken breast on the bottom of a roll and close with its top, repeating as necessary to make additional sandwiches. Serve warm.

Variations & Ingredients Tips:

- Substitute the Brie with Camembert or another soft cheese of your choice.
- Use pears instead of apples for a different flavor profile.
- Add baby spinach or arugula for extra greens and nutrition.

Per Serving: Calories: 510; Cholesterol: 135mg; Total Fat: 19g; Saturated Fat: 8g; Sodium: 670mg; Total Carbohydrates: 41g; Dietary Fiber: 2g; Total Sugars: 6g; Protein: 45g

Chicken Gyros

Servings: 4 | Prep Time: 10 Minutes (plus Marinating Time) | Cooking Time: 14 Minutes

Ingredients:

- 4 110to 140-gram boneless skinless chicken thighs, trimmed of any fat blobs
- 2 tablespoons Lemon juice
- 2 tablespoons Red wine vinegar
- 2 tablespoons Olive oil
- 2 teaspoons Dried oregano
- 2 teaspoons Minced garlic
- 1 teaspoon Table salt
- 1 teaspoon Ground black pepper
- 4 Pita pockets (gluten-free, if a concern)
- ½ cup Chopped tomatoes
- ½ cup Bottled regular, low-fat, or fat-free ranch dressing (gluten-free, if a concern)

Directions:

1. Mix the thighs, lemon juice, vinegar, oil, oregano, garlic, salt, and pepper in a zip-closed bag. Seal, gently massage the marinade into the meat through the plastic, and refrigerate for at least 2 hours or up to 6 hours. (Longer than that and the meat can turn rubbery.)
2. Set the plastic bag out on the counter (to make the contents a little less frigid). Preheat the air fryer to 190°C/375°F.
3. When the machine is at temperature, use kitchen tongs to place the thighs in the basket in one layer. Discard the marinade. Air-fry the chicken thighs undisturbed for 12 minutes, or until browned and an instant-read meat thermometer inserted into the thickest part of one thigh registers 75°C/165°F. You may need to air-fry the chicken 2 minutes longer if the machine's temperature is 70°C/360°F.
4. Use kitchen tongs to transfer the thighs to a cutting board. Cool for 5 minutes, then set one thigh in each of the pita pockets. Top each with 2 tablespoons chopped tomatoes and 2 tablespoons dressing. Serve warm.

Variations & Ingredients Tips:

- Substitute chicken thighs with chicken breast for a leaner option.
- Add shredded lettuce, sliced onions, or cucumbers for extra crunch and flavor.
- Use homemade tzatziki sauce instead of ranch dressing for

a more authentic taste.

Per Serving: Calories: 460; Cholesterol: 95mg; Total Fat: 28g; Saturated Fat: 5g; Sodium: 1070mg; Total Carbohydrates: 29g; Dietary Fiber: 2g; Total Sugars: 4g; Protein: 25g

Appetizers And Snacks

Caponata Salsa

Servings: 6 | Prep Time: 10 Minutes | Cooking Time: 16 Minutes

Ingredients:

- 4 cups (450 g eggplant) Purple Italian eggplant(s), stemmed and diced (no need to peel)
- Olive oil spray
- 1½ cups Celery, thinly sliced
- 16 (about 225 g) Cherry or grape tomatoes, halved
- 1 tablespoon Drained and rinsed capers,
- chopped
- Up to 1 tablespoon Minced fresh rosemary leaves
- 1½ tablespoons Red wine vinegar
- 1½ teaspoons Granulated white sugar
- ¾ teaspoon Table salt
- ¾ teaspoon Ground black pepper

Directions:

1. Preheat the air fryer to 175°C/350°F.
2. Put the eggplant pieces in a bowl and generously coat them with olive oil spray. Toss and stir, spray again, and toss some more, until the pieces are glistening.
3. When the machine is at temperature, pour the eggplant pieces into the basket and spread them out into an even layer. Air-fry for 8 minutes, tossing and rearranging the pieces twice.
4. Meanwhile, put the celery and tomatoes in the same bowl the eggplant pieces had been in. Generously coat them with olive oil spray; then toss well, spray again, and toss some more, until the vegetables are well coated.
5. When the eggplant has cooked for 8 minutes, pour the celery and tomatoes on top in the basket. Air-fry undisturbed for 8 minutes more, until the tomatoes have begun to soften.
6. Pour the contents of the basket back into the same bowl. Add the capers, rosemary, vinegar, sugar, salt, and pepper. Toss well to blend, breaking up the tomatoes a bit to create more moisture in the mixture.
7. Cover and refrigerate for 2 hours to blend the flavors. Serve chilled or at room temperature. The caponata salsa can stay in its covered bowl in the fridge for up to 2 days before the vegetables weep too much moisture and the dish becomes too wet.

Variations & Ingredients Tips:

- Add some chopped olives, pine nuts or raisins for extra flavor and texture.
- Drizzle with balsamic glaze before serving.
- Serve as a topping for crostini, bruschetta or grilled meats.

Per Serving: Calories: 103; Total Fat: 3g; Saturated Fat: 0g; Cholesterol: 0mg; Sodium: 419mg; Total Carbs: 19g; Dietary Fiber: 6g; Total Sugars: 11g; Protein: 3g

Cheesy Pigs In A Blanket

Servings: 4 | Prep Time: 15 Minutes | Cooking Time: 7 Minutes

Ingredients:

- 24 cocktail size smoked sausages
- 6 slices deli-sliced Cheddar cheese, each cut into 8 rectangular pieces
- 1 (225 g) tube refrigerated crescent roll dough
- ketchup or mustard for dipping

Directions:

1. Unroll the crescent roll dough into one large sheet. If your crescent roll dough has perforated seams, pinch or roll all the perforated seams together. Cut the large sheet of dough into 4 rectangles. Then cut each rectangle into 6 pieces by making one slice lengthwise in the middle and 2 slices horizontally. You should have 24 pieces of dough.
2. Make a deep slit lengthwise down the center of the cocktail sausage. Stuff two pieces of cheese into the slit in the sausage. Roll one piece of crescent dough around the stuffed cocktail sausage leaving the ends of the sausage exposed. Pinch the seam together. Repeat with the remaining sausages.
3. Preheat the air fryer to 175°C/350°F.
4. Air-fry in 2 batches, placing the sausages seam side down in the basket. Air-fry for 7 minutes. Serve hot with ketchup or your favorite mustard for dipping.

Variations & Ingredients Tips:

- Use bratwurst or Italian sausage instead of smoked sausage.
- Stuff with pepper jack or mozzarella cheese for different flavors.
- Brush with melted butter and sprinkle with everything bagel seasoning before cooking.

Per Serving: Calories: 469; Total Fat: 37g; Saturated Fat: 14g; Cholesterol: 55mg; Sodium: 1315mg; Total Carbs: 21g; Dietary Fiber: 0g; Total Sugars: 6g; Protein: 16g

Crispy Chicken Bites With Gorgonzola Sauce

Servings: 4 | Prep Time: 15 Minutes | Cooking Time: 30 Minutes

Ingredients:

- ¼ cup crumbled Gorgonzola cheese
- ¼ cup creamy blue cheese salad dressing
- 450 g chicken tenders, cut into thirds crosswise
- ½ cup sour cream
- 1 celery stalk, chopped
- 3 tbsp buffalo chicken sauce
- 1 cup panko bread crumbs
- 2 tbsp olive oil

Directions:

1. Preheat air fryer to 175°C/350°F. Blend together sour cream, salad dressing, Gorgonzola cheese, and celery in a bowl. Set aside. Combine chicken pieces and Buffalo wing sauce in another bowl until the chicken is coated.
2. In a shallow bowl or pie plate, mix the bread crumbs and olive oil. Dip the chicken into the bread crumb mixture, patting the crumbs to keep them in place. Arrange the chicken in the greased frying basket and Air Fry for 8-9 minutes, shaking once halfway through cooking until the chicken is golden. Serve with the blue cheese sauce.

Variations & Ingredients Tips:

- Use boneless skinless chicken thighs instead of tenders.
- Substitute ranch dressing for the blue cheese dressing.
- Add some garlic powder or onion powder to the bread crumb mixture.

Per Serving: Calories: 446; Total Fat: 27g; Saturated Fat: 10g; Cholesterol: 92mg; Sodium: 815mg; Total Carbs: 19g; Dietary Fiber: 1g; Total Sugars: 3g; Protein: 32g

Cheddar-pimiento Strips | Prep Time: 15 Minutes | Servings: 4

Cooking Time: 35 Minutes

Ingredients:

- 225 g shredded sharp cheddar cheese
- 1 jar chopped pimientos, including juice
- ¼ cup mayonnaise
- ¼ cup cream cheese
- Salt and pepper to taste
- 1 tsp chopped parsley
- 8 slices sandwich bread
- 4 tbsp butter, melted

Directions:

1. In a bowl, mix the cheddar cheese, cream cheese, pimientos, mayonnaise, salt, parsley and pepper. Let chill covered in the fridge for 30 minutes.
2. Preheat air fryer at 175°C/350°F. Spread pimiento mixture over 4 bread slices, then top with the remaining slices and press down just enough to not smoosh cheese out of sandwiches edges. Brush the top and bottom of each sandwich lightly with melted butter. Place sandwiches in the frying basket and Grill for 6 minutes, flipping once. Slice each sandwich into 16 sections and serve warm.

Variations & Ingredients Tips:

- Use sourdough or rye bread for a tangy flavor.
- Add some chopped green onions or diced jalapenos to the cheese mixture.
- Serve with tomato soup or a green salad on the side.

Per Serving: Calories: 609; Total Fat: 46g; Saturated Fat: 25g; Cholesterol: 97mg; Sodium: 1040mg; Total Carbs: 30g; Dietary Fiber: 2g; Total Sugars: 5g; Protein: 22g

Corn Dog Bites

Servings: 3 | Prep Time: 20 Minutes | Cooking Time: 12 Minutes

Ingredients:

- 3 cups Purchased cornbread stuffing mix
- ⅓ cup All-purpose flour
- 2 Large egg(s), well beaten
- 3 Hot dogs, cut into 5 cm pieces (vegetarian hot dogs, if preferred)
- Vegetable oil spray

Directions:

1. Preheat the air fryer to 190°C/375°F.
2. Put the cornbread stuffing mix in a food processor. Cover and pulse to grind into a mixture like fine bread crumbs.
3. Set up and fill three shallow soup plates or small pie plates on your counter: one for the flour, one for the egg(s), and one for the stuffing mix crumbs.
4. Dip a hot dog piece in the flour to coat it completely, then gently shake off any excess. Dip the hot dog piece into the egg(s) and gently roll it around to coat all surfaces, then pick it up and allow any excess egg to slip back into the rest. Set the hot dog piece in the stuffing mix crumbs and roll it gently to coat it evenly and well on all sides, even the ends. Set it aside on a cutting board and continue dipping and coating the remaining hot dog pieces.
5. Give the coated hot dog pieces a generous coating of veg-

etable oil spray on all sides, then set them in the basket in one layer with some space between them. Air-fry undisturbed for 10 minutes, or until golden brown and crunchy. (You'll need to add 2 minutes in the air fryer if the temperature is at 180°C/360°F.)

6. Use a nonstick-safe spatula, and perhaps a flatware fork for balance, to transfer the corn dog bites to a wire rack. Cool for 5 minutes before serving.

Variations & Ingredients Tips:

- Use Italian sausage, kielbasa or andouille instead of hot dogs.
- Roll the coated pieces in crushed pretzels or potato chips before air frying.
- Serve with honey mustard, spicy ketchup or cheese sauce for dipping.

Per Serving: Calories: 441; Total Fat: 21g; Saturated Fat: 6g; Cholesterol: 106mg; Sodium: 1451mg; Total Carbs: 50g; Dietary Fiber: 2g; Total Sugars: 6g; Protein: 14g

Popcorn Chicken Bites

Servings: 2 | Prep Time: 10 Minutes + Marinating Time | Cooking Time: 8 Minutes

Ingredients:

- 450 g chicken breasts, cutlets or tenders
- 1 cup buttermilk
- 3 to 6 dashes hot sauce (optional)
- 8 cups cornflakes (or 2
- cups cornflake crumbs)
- ½ tsp salt
- 1 tbsp butter, melted
- 2 tbsp chopped fresh parsley

Directions:

1. Cut the chicken into bite-sized pieces (about 2.5 cm) and place them in a bowl with the buttermilk and hot sauce (if using). Cover and let the chicken marinate in the buttermilk for 1 to 3 hours in the refrigerator. Preheat the air fryer to 190°C/380°F. Crush the cornflakes into fine crumbs by either crushing them with your hands in a bowl, rolling them with a rolling pin in a plastic bag or processing them in a food processor. Place the crumbs in a bowl, add the salt, melted butter and parsley and mix well. Working in batches, remove the chicken from the buttermilk marinade, letting any excess drip off and transfer the chicken to the cornflakes. Toss the chicken pieces in the cornflake mixture to coat evenly, pressing the crumbs onto the chicken. Air-fry the chicken in two batches for 8 minutes per batch, shaking the basket halfway through the cooking process. Re-heat the first batch with the second batch for a couple of minutes if desired. Serve the popcorn chicken bites warm with BBQ sauce or honey mustard for dipping.

Variations & Ingredients Tips:

- Use panko breadcrumbs or crushed pretzels instead of

cornflakes for a different texture.
- Add dried herbs, spices, or grated Parmesan cheese to the cornflake mixture for extra flavor.
- Make a spicy version by adding more hot sauce to the buttermilk marinade or cayenne pepper to the cornflake coating.

Per Serving: Calories: 487; Total Fat: 16g; Saturated Fat: 6g; Cholesterol: 145mg; Sodium: 1012mg; Total Carbs: 43g; Dietary Fiber: 1g; Total Sugars: 10g; Protein: 45g

Hot Cauliflower Bites

Servings: 4 | Prep Time: 15 Minutes | Cooking Time: 35 Minutes

Ingredients:

- 1 head cauliflower, cut into florets
- 1 cup all-purpose flour
- 1 tsp garlic powder
- 1/3 cup cayenne sauce

Directions:

1. Preheat air fryer to 190°C/370°F. Mix the flour, 1 cup of water, and garlic powder in a large bowl until a batter forms. Coat cauliflower in the batter, then transfer to a large bowl to drain excess. Place the cauliflower in the greased frying basket without stacking. Spray with cooking, then Bake for 6 minutes. Remove from the air fryer and transfer to a large bowl. Top with cayenne sauce. Return to the fryer and cook for 6 minutes or until crispy. Serve.

Variations & Ingredients Tips:

- Use broccoli florets or zucchini chunks instead of cauliflower.
- Toss the cooked bites with buffalo sauce, BBQ sauce or teriyaki glaze.
- Serve with blue cheese dressing or ranch dip on the side.

Per Serving: Calories: 154; Total Fat: 1g; Saturated Fat: 0g; Cholesterol: 0mg; Sodium: 613mg; Total Carbs: 33g; Dietary Fiber: 5g; Total Sugars: 3g; Protein: 6g

Brie-currant & Bacon Spread

Servings: 6 | Prep Time: 10 Minutes | Cooking Time: 30 Minutes

Ingredients:

- 113 g cream cheese, softened
- 3 tbsp mayonnaise
- 1 cup diced Brie cheese
- ½ tsp dried thyme
- 113 g cooked bacon, crumbled
- 1/3 cup dried currants

Directions:

1. Preheat the air fryer to 175°C/350°F. Beat the cream cheese

with the mayo until well blended. Stir in the Brie, thyme, bacon, and currants and pour the dip mix in a 15 cm round pan. Put the pan in the fryer and Air Fry for 10-12 minutes, stirring once until the dip is melting and bubbling. Serve warm.

Variations & Ingredients Tips:

- Substitute dried cranberries or apricots for the currants.
- Add some chopped nuts like pecans or walnuts for crunch.
- Serve with sliced baguette, crackers or apple slices for dipping.

Per Serving: Calories: 290; Total Fat: 24g; Saturated Fat: 11g; Cholesterol: 63mg; Sodium: 486mg; Total Carbs: 9g; Dietary Fiber: 1g; Total Sugars: 6g; Protein: 11g

Sweet Potato Fries With Sweet And Spicy Dipping Sauce

Servings: 2 | Prep Time: 10 Minutes | Cooking Time: 20 Minutes

Ingredients:

- 1 large sweet potato (about 450 g)
- 1 tsp vegetable or canola oil
- salt
- Sweet & Spicy Dipping Sauce
- ¼ cup light mayonnaise
- 1 tbsp spicy brown mustard
- 1 tbsp sweet Thai chili sauce
- ½ tsp sriracha sauce

Directions:

1. Scrub the sweet potato well and then cut it into 6-mm French fries. (A mandolin slicer can really help with this.) Preheat the air fryer to 95°C/200°F. Toss the sweet potato sticks with the oil and transfer them to the air fryer basket. Air-fry at 95°C/200°F for 10 minutes, shaking the basket several times during the cooking process for even cooking. Toss the fries with salt, increase the air fryer temperature to 200°C/400°F and air-fry for another 10 minutes, shaking the basket several times during the cooking process. To make the dipping sauce, combine all the ingredients in a small bowl and stir until combined. Serve the sweet potato fries warm with the dipping sauce on the side.

Variations & Ingredients Tips:

- Experiment with different seasonings like paprika, garlic powder, or Old Bay seasoning for extra flavor.
- Add a squeeze of lime juice or a pinch of cayenne pepper to the dipping sauce for more tang and heat.
- Serve with ketchup, ranch dressing, or honey mustard for dipping variety.

Per Serving: Calories: 258; Total Fat: 12g; Saturated Fat: 2g; Cholesterol: 8mg; Sodium: 679mg; Total Carbohydrates: 35g; Dietary Fiber: 5g; Total Sugars: 11g; Protein: 3g

Fried Goat Cheese

Servings: 3 | Prep Time: 40 Minutes | Cooking Time: 4 Minutes

Ingredients:

- 200 g 2.5 to 4 cm diameter goat cheese log
- 2 Large egg(s)
- 1¾ cups Plain dried
- bread crumbs (gluten-free, if a concern)
- Vegetable oil spray

Directions:

1. Slice the goat cheese log into 13 mm thick rounds. Set these flat on a small cutting board, a small baking sheet, or a large plate. Freeze uncovered for 30 minutes.
2. Preheat the air fryer to 200°C/400°F.
3. Set up and fill two shallow soup plates or small pie plates on your counter: one in which you whisk the egg(s) until uniform and the other for the bread crumbs.
4. Take the goat cheese rounds out of the freezer. With clean, dry hands, dip one round in the egg(s) to coat it on all sides. Let the excess egg slip back into the rest, then dredge the round in the bread crumbs, turning it to coat all sides, even the edges. Repeat this process—egg, then bread crumbs—for a second coating. Coat both sides of the round and its edges with vegetable oil spray, then set it aside. Continue double-dipping, double-dredging, and spraying the remaining rounds.
5. Place the rounds in one layer in the basket. Air-fry undisturbed for 4 minutes, or until lightly browned and crunchy. Do not overcook. Some of the goat cheese may break through the crust. A few little breaks are fine but stop the cooking before the coating reaches structural failure.
6. Remove the basket from the machine and set aside for 3 minutes. Use a nonstick-safe spatula, and maybe a flatware fork for balance, to transfer the rounds to a wire rack. Cool for 5 minutes more before serving.

Variations & Ingredients Tips:

- Use brie, camembert or feta instead of goat cheese.
- Roll the breaded rounds in chopped nuts, herbs or seeds before air frying.
- Serve with honey, fig jam or cranberry sauce for dipping.

Per Serving: Calories: 490; Total Fat: 24g; Saturated Fat: 12g; Cholesterol: 174mg; Sodium: 935mg; Total Carbs: 44g; Dietary Fiber: 3g; Total Sugars: 5g; Protein: 26g

Sweet-and-salty Pretzels

Servings: 4 | Prep Time: 5 Minutes | Cooking Time: 5 Minutes

Ingredients:

- 2 cups plain pretzel nug-   gets

- 1 tbsp Worcestershire sauce
- 2 tsp granulated white sugar
- 1 tsp mild smoked paprika
- ½ tsp garlic or onion powder

Directions:

1. Preheat the air fryer to 175°C/350°F. Put the pretzel nuggets, Worcestershire sauce, sugar, smoked paprika, and garlic or onion powder in a large bowl. Toss gently until the nuggets are well coated. When the machine is at temperature, pour the nuggets into the basket, spreading them into as close to a single layer as possible. Air-fry, shaking the basket three or four times to rearrange the nuggets, for 5 minutes, or until the nuggets are toasted and aromatic. Although the coating will darken, don't let it burn, especially if the machine's temperature is 180°C/360°F. Pour the nuggets onto a wire rack and gently spread them into one layer. (A rubber spatula does a good job.) Cool for 5 minutes before serving.

Variations & Ingredients Tips:

- Experiment with different spice blends like ranch seasoning, taco seasoning, or Italian herbs.
- Add a pinch of cayenne pepper or red pepper flakes for a spicy kick.
- Drizzle with melted chocolate or caramel for a sweet and salty treat.

Per Serving: Calories: 113; Total Fat: 1g; Saturated Fat: 0g; Sodium: 504mg; Total Carbohydrates: 24g; Dietary Fiber: 1g; Total Sugars: 3g; Protein: 3g

Dill Fried Pickles With Light Ranch Dip

Servings: 4 | Prep Time: 15 Minutes | Cooking Time: 8 Minutes

Ingredients:

- 4 to 6 large dill pickles, sliced in half or quartered lengthwise
- ½ cup all-purpose flour
- 2 eggs, lightly beaten
- 1 cup plain breadcrumbs
- 1 teaspoon salt
- ⅛ teaspoon cayenne pepper
- 2 tablespoons fresh dill leaves, dried well
- vegetable oil, in a spray bottle
- Light Ranch Dip
- ¼ cup reduced-fat mayonnaise
- ¼ cup buttermilk
- ¼ cup non-fat Greek yogurt
- 1 tablespoon chopped fresh chives
- 1 tablespoon chopped fresh parsley
- 1 tablespoon lemon juice
- salt and freshly ground black pepper

Directions:

1. Dry the dill pickle spears very well with a clean kitchen towel.
2. Set up a dredging station using three shallow dishes. Place the flour in the first shallow dish. Place the eggs into the second dish. Combine the breadcrumbs, salt, cayenne and fresh dill in a food processor and process until everything is combined and the crumbs are very fine. Place the crumb mixture in the third dish.
3. Preheat the air fryer to 200°C/400°F.
4. Coat the pickles by dredging them first in the flour, then the egg, and then the breadcrumbs, pressing the crumbs on gently with your hands. Set the coated pickles on a tray and spray them on all sides with vegetable oil.
5. Air-fry one layer of pickles at a time at 200°C/400°F for 8 minutes, turning them over halfway through the cooking process and spraying lightly again if necessary. The crumbs should be nicely browned on all sides.
6. While the pickles are air-frying, make the light ranch dip by mixing everything together in a bowl. Serve the pickles warm with the dip on the side.

Variations & Ingredients Tips:

- Use zucchini spears or green beans instead of pickles.
- Add some garlic powder, onion powder or smoked paprika to the breading.
- Serve with blue cheese dressing or spicy remoulade for dipping.

Per Serving: Calories: 245; Total Fat: 8g; Saturated Fat: 2g; Cholesterol: 98mg; Sodium: 1549mg; Total Carbs: 33g; Dietary Fiber: 2g; Total Sugars: 5g; Protein: 10g

Tempura Fried Veggies

Servings: 4 | Prep Time: 20 Minutes | Cooking Time: 6 Minutes

Ingredients:

- ½ cup all-purpose flour
- ½ tsp black pepper
- ¼ tsp salt
- 2 large eggs
- 1¼ cups panko breadcrumbs
- 1 tbsp extra-virgin olive oil
- 1 cup white button mushrooms, cleaned
- 1 medium zucchini, skinned and sliced
- 1 medium carrot, skinned sliced

Directions:

1. Preheat the air fryer to 200°C/400°F. In a small bowl, mix the flour, pepper, and salt. In a separate bowl, whisk the eggs. In a third bowl, mix together the breadcrumbs and olive oil. Begin to batter the vegetables by placing them one at a time into the flour, then dipping them in the eggs, and coating them in breadcrumbs. When you've prepared enough to begin air frying, liberally spray the air fryer basket with olive oil and place the vegetables inside. Cook for 6 minutes, or until the breadcrumb coating on the outside appears golden brown. Repeat coating the other vegetables while the first batch is cooking. When the cooking completes, carefully remove the vegetables and keep them

warm. Repeat cooking for the remaining vegetables until all are cooked. Serve warm.

Variations & Ingredients Tips:

- Experiment with different vegetables like broccoli, cauliflower, bell peppers, or sweet potatoes.
- Add garlic powder, onion powder, or smoked paprika to the flour mixture for extra seasoning.
- Serve with tempura dipping sauce, soy sauce, or sweet chili sauce for added flavor.

Per Serving: Calories: 240; Total Fat: 9g; Saturated Fat: 2g; Cholesterol: 93mg; Sodium: 371mg; Total Carbohydrates: 31g; Dietary Fiber: 2g; Total Sugars: 3g; Protein: 9g

Indian Cauliflower Tikka Bites

Servings: 6 | Prep Time: 15 Minutes | Cooking Time: 20 Minutes

Ingredients:

- 1 cup plain Greek yogurt
- 1 teaspoon fresh ginger
- 1 teaspoon minced garlic
- 1 teaspoon vindaloo
- ½ teaspoon cardamom
- ½ teaspoon paprika
- ½ teaspoon turmeric powder
- ½ teaspoon cumin powder
- 1 large head of cauliflower, washed and cut into medium-size florets
- ½ cup panko breadcrumbs
- 1 lemon, quartered

Directions:

1. Preheat the air fryer to 175°C/350°F.
2. In a large bowl, mix the yogurt, ginger, garlic, vindaloo, cardamom, paprika, turmeric, and cumin. Add the cauliflower florets to the bowl, and coat them with the yogurt.
3. Remove the cauliflower florets from the bowl and place them on a baking sheet. Sprinkle the panko breadcrumbs over the top. Place the cauliflower bites into the air fryer basket, leaving space between the florets. Depending on the size of your air fryer, you may need to make more than one batch.
4. Cook the cauliflower for 10 minutes, shake the basket, and continue cooking another 10 minutes (or until the florets are lightly browned).
5. Remove from the air fryer and keep warm. Continue to cook until all the florets are done.
6. Before serving, lightly squeeze lemon over the top. Serve warm.

Variations & Ingredients Tips:

- Use broccoli or zucchini instead of cauliflower for different vegetables.
- Add some chopped cilantro or mint to the yogurt marinade.
- Serve with mango chutney or raita yogurt sauce for dipping.

Per Serving: Calories: 101; Total Fat: 2g; Saturated Fat: 1g; Cholesterol: 5mg; Sodium: 103mg; Total Carbs: 14g; Dietary Fiber: 3g; Total Sugars: 4g; Protein: 7g

Mediterranean Potato Skins

Servings: 4 | Prep Time: 10 Minutes | Cooking Time: 50 Minutes

Ingredients:

- 2 russet potatoes
- 3 tbsp olive oil
- Salt and pepper to taste
- 2 tbsp rosemary, chopped
- 10 Kalamata olives, diced
- ¼ cup crumbled feta
- 2 tbsp chopped dill

Directions:

1. Preheat air fryer to 190°C/380°F. Poke 2-3 holes in the potatoes with a fork. Drizzle them with some olive oil and sprinkle with salt. Put the potatoes into the frying basket and bake for 30 minutes. When the potatoes are ready, remove them from the fryer and slice in half. Scoop out the flesh of the potatoes with a spoon, leaving a 3-cm layer of potato inside the skins, and set the skins aside. Combine the scooped potato middles with the remaining olive oil, salt, black pepper, and rosemary in a medium bowl. Mix until well combined. Spoon the potato filling into the potato skins, spreading it evenly over them. Top with olives, dill, and feta. Put the loaded potato skins back into the air fryer and bake for 15 minutes. Enjoy!

Variations & Ingredients Tips:

- Add sun-dried tomatoes, artichokes, or roasted red peppers for more Mediterranean flavors.
- Substitute feta with goat cheese or ricotta salata for a different taste.
- Sprinkle with smoked paprika or red pepper flakes for a spicy kick.

Per Serving: Calories: 257; Total Fat: 18g; Saturated Fat: 4g; Cholesterol: 17mg; Sodium: 327mg; Total Carbs: 21g; Dietary Fiber: 2g; Total Sugars: 1g; Protein: 5g

Yellow Onion Rings

Servings: 3 | Prep Time: 15 Minutes | Cooking Time: 30 Minutes

Ingredients:

- ½ sweet yellow onion
- ½ cup buttermilk
- ¾ cup flour
- 1 tbsp cornstarch
- Salt and pepper to taste
- ¾ tsp garlic powder
- ½ tsp dried oregano
- 1 cup bread crumbs

Directions:

Preheat air fryer to 200°C/390°F. Cut the onion into 3-cm slices. Separate the onion slices into rings. Place the buttermilk in a bowl and set aside. In another bowl, combine the flour, cornstarch, salt, pepper, and garlic. Stir well and set aside. In a separate bowl, combine the breadcrumbs with oregano and salt. Dip the rings into the buttermilk, dredge in flour, dip into the buttermilk again, and then coat into the crumb mixture. Put in the greased frying basket without overlapping. Spritz them with cooking oil and air fry for 13-16 minutes, shaking once or twice until the rings are crunchy and browned. Serve hot.

Variations & Ingredients Tips:

- Add smoked paprika, cayenne pepper, or chili powder to the flour mixture for a spicy kick.
- Use panko breadcrumbs or crushed potato chips for a crunchier coating.
- Serve with ranch dressing, honey mustard, or BBQ sauce for dipping.

Per Serving: Calories: 331; Total Fat: 4g; Saturated Fat: 1g; Cholesterol: 2mg; Sodium: 277mg; Total Carbohydrates: 65g; Dietary Fiber: 4g; Total Sugars: 7g; Protein: 11g

Orange-glazed Carrots

Servings: 3 | Prep Time: 10 Minutes | Cooking Time: 25 Minutes

Ingredients:

- 3 carrots, cut into spears
- 1 tbsp orange juice
- 2 tsp balsamic vinegar
- 1 tsp avocado oil
- 1 tsp clear honey
- ½ tsp dried rosemary
- ¼ tsp salt
- ¼ tsp lemon zest

Directions:

Preheat air fryer to 200°C/390°F. Put the carrots in a baking pan. Add the orange juice, balsamic vinegar, oil, honey, rosemary, salt, and zest. Stir well. Roast for 15-18 minutes, shaking them once or twice until the carrots are bright orange, glazed, and tender. Serve while hot.

Variations & Ingredients Tips:

- Use maple syrup or agave nectar instead of honey for a vegan version.
- Add a pinch of cayenne pepper or red pepper flakes for a spicy kick.
- Sprinkle with chopped fresh parsley or mint before serving for a pop of color and freshness.

Per Serving: Calories: 69; Total Fat: 2g; Saturated Fat: 0g; Cholesterol: no data; Sodium: 222mg; Total Carbs: 12g; Dietary Fiber: 2g; Total Sugars: 8g; Protein: 1g

Homemade Pretzel Bites

Servings: 8 | Prep Time: 90 Minutes | Cooking Time: 10 Minutes

Ingredients:

- 1.2 L filtered water, divided
- 1 tablespoon butter
- 1 package fast-rising yeast
- ½ teaspoon salt
- 2⅓ cups bread flour
- 2 tablespoons baking soda
- 2 egg whites
- 1 teaspoon kosher salt

Directions:

1. Preheat the air fryer to 190°C/370°F.
2. In a large microwave-safe bowl, add 180 ml of the water. Heat for 40 seconds in the microwave. Remove and whisk in the butter; then mix in the yeast and salt. Let sit 5 minutes.
3. Using a stand mixer with a dough hook attachment, add the yeast liquid and mix in the bread flour 80 ml at a time until all the flour is added and a dough is formed.
4. Remove the bowl from the stand; then let the dough rise 1 hour in a warm space, covered with a kitchen towel.
5. After the dough has doubled in size, remove from the bowl and punch down a few times on a lightly floured flat surface.
6. Divide the dough into 4 balls; then roll each ball out into a long, skinny, sticklike shape. Using a sharp knife, cut each dough stick into 6 pieces.
7. Repeat Step 6 for the remaining dough balls until you have about 24 bites formed.
8. Heat the remaining 950 ml of water over the stovetop in a medium pot with the baking soda stirred in.
9. Drop the pretzel bite dough into the hot water and let boil for 60 seconds, remove, and let slightly cool.
10. Lightly brush the top of each bite with the egg whites, and then cover with a pinch of kosher salt.
11. Spray the air fryer basket with olive oil spray and place the pretzel bites on top. Cook for 6 to 8 minutes, or until lightly browned. Remove and keep warm.
12. Repeat until all pretzel bites are cooked.
13. Serve warm.

Variations & Ingredients Tips:

- Add some cinnamon sugar, everything bagel seasoning or Parmesan cheese to the egg wash.
- Serve with mustard, cheese sauce or beer cheese dip for dunking.
- Make pretzel dogs by wrapping the dough around hot dogs before boiling and baking.

Per Serving: Calories: 203; Total Fat: 2g; Saturated Fat: 1g; Cholesterol: 4mg; Sodium: 1783mg; Total Carbs: 39g; Dietary Fiber: 1g; Total Sugars: 0g; Protein: 7g

Charred Shishito Peppers

Servings: 4 | Prep Time: 5 Minutes | Cooking Time: 5 Minutes

Ingredients:

- 170 g shishito peppers (about 170-g)
- 1 teaspoon vegetable oil
- coarse sea salt
- 1 lemon

Directions:

1. Preheat the air fryer to 195°C/390°F.
2. Toss the shishito peppers with the oil and salt. You can do this in a bowl or directly in the air fryer basket.
3. Air-fry at 195°C/390°F for 5 minutes, shaking the basket once or twice while they cook.
4. Turn the charred peppers out into a bowl. Squeeze some lemon juice over the top and season with coarse sea salt. These should be served as finger foods – pick the pepper up by the stem and eat the whole pepper, seeds and all. Watch for that surprise spicy one!

Variations & Ingredients Tips:

- Use padron peppers instead of shishitos for a Spanish twist.
- Sprinkle with togarashi or furikake seasoning for an Asian flair.
- Serve with a soy-ginger dipping sauce on the side.

Per Serving: Calories: 27; Total Fat: 2g; Saturated Fat: 0g; Cholesterol: 0mg; Sodium: 80mg; Total Carbs: 2g; Dietary Fiber: 1g; Total Sugars: 1g; Protein: 1g

Cheesy Tortellini Bites

Servings: 8 | Prep Time: 15 Minutes | Cooking Time: 10 Minutes

Ingredients:

- 1 large egg
- ½ teaspoon black pepper
- ½ teaspoon garlic powder
- 1 teaspoon Italian seasoning
- 340 g frozen cheese tortellini
- ½ cup panko breadcrumbs

Directions:

1. Preheat the air fryer to 190°C/380°F.
2. Spray the air fryer basket with an olive-oil-based spray.
3. In a medium bowl, whisk the egg with the pepper, garlic powder, and Italian seasoning.
4. Dip the tortellini in the egg batter and then coat with the breadcrumbs. Place each tortellini in the basket, trying not to overlap them. You may need to cook in batches to ensure the even crisp all around.
5. Bake for 5 minutes, shake the basket, and bake another 5 minutes.
6. Remove and let cool 5 minutes. Serve with marinara sauce, ranch, or your favorite dressing.

Variations & Ingredients Tips:

- Use ravioli, gnocchi or mini pierogi instead of tortellini.
- Add some grated Parmesan to the breadcrumbs for extra flavor.
- Stuff the tortellini with a small piece of mozzarella before breading.

Per Serving: Calories: 169; Total Fat: 4g; Saturated Fat: 2g; Cholesterol: 40mg; Sodium: 282mg; Total Carbs: 24g; Dietary Fiber: 1g; Total Sugars: 1g; Protein: 8g

Vegetable Side Dishes Recipes

Corn Au Gratin

Servings: 4 | Prep Time: 10 Minutes | Cooking Time: 20 Minutes

Ingredients:

- ½ cup grated cheddar
- 3 tbsp flour
- 2 cups yellow corn
- 1 egg, beaten
- ¼ cup milk
- ½ cup heavy cream
- Salt and pepper to taste
- 2 tbsp butter, cubed

Directions:

1. Preheat air fryer to 160°C/320°F.
2. Mix flour, corn, egg, milk, and heavy cream in a medium bowl.
3. Stir in cheddar cheese, salt and pepper.
4. Pour into a prepared baking pan.
5. Top with butter cubes.
6. Bake for 15 minutes.
7. Serve warm.

Variations & Ingredients Tips:

- Add diced jalapeños or green chiles for a kick.
- Substitute cream of mushroom or chicken soup for the milk and cream.
- Top with panko breadcrumbs before baking for a crispy topping.

Per Serving: Calories: 380; Total Fat: 28g; Saturated Fat: 16g; Cholesterol: 125mg; Sodium: 260mg; Total Carbs: 24g; Fiber: 2g; Sugars: 5g; Protein: 10g

Yellow Squash

Servings: 4 | Prep Time: 15 Minutes | Cooking Time: 10 Minutes

Ingredients:

- 1 large yellow squash (about 1½ cups)
- 2 eggs
- ¼ cup buttermilk
- 1 cup panko bread-
- crumbs
- ¼ cup white cornmeal
- ½ tsp salt
- oil for misting or cooking spray

Directions:

1. Preheat air fryer to 200°C/390°F. Cut the squash into 6-mm slices. In a shallow dish, beat together eggs and buttermilk. In a sealable plastic bag or container with lid, combine ¼ cup panko crumbs, white cornmeal, and salt. Shake to mix well. Place the remaining ¾ cup panko crumbs in a separate shallow dish. Dump all the squash slices into the egg/buttermilk mixture. Stir to coat. Remove squash from buttermilk mixture with a slotted spoon, letting excess drip off, and transfer to the panko/cornmeal mixture. Close bag or container and shake well to coat. Remove squash from crumb mixture, letting excess fall off. Return squash to egg/buttermilk mixture, stirring gently to coat. If you need more liquid to coat all the squash, add a little more buttermilk. Remove each squash slice from egg wash and dip in a dish of ¾ cup panko crumbs. Mist squash slices with oil or cooking spray and place in air fryer basket. Squash should be in a single layer, but it's okay if the slices crowd together and overlap a little. Cook at 200°C/390°F for 5 minutes. Shake basket to break up any that have stuck together. Mist again with oil or spray. Cook 5 minutes longer and check. If necessary, mist again with oil and cook an additional two minutes, until squash slices are golden brown and crisp.

Variations & Ingredients Tips:

- Use zucchini, eggplant, or green tomatoes instead of yellow squash for different veggie options.
- Add garlic powder, onion powder, or smoked paprika to the cornmeal mixture for extra seasoning.
- Serve with ranch dressing, marinara sauce, or lemon aioli for dipping.

Per Serving: Calories: 180; Total Fat: 6g; Saturated Fat: 2g; Cholesterol: 93mg; Sodium: 490mg; Total Carbohydrates: 25g; Dietary Fiber: 2g; Total Sugars: 3g; Protein: 7g

Carrots & Parsnips With Tahini Sauce

Servings: 4 | Prep Time: 10 Minutes | Cooking Time: 20 Minutes

Ingredients:

- 2 parsnips, cut into half-moons
- 2 tsp olive oil
- ½ tsp salt
- 1 carrot, cut into sticks
- 1 tbsp tahini
- 1 tbsp lemon juice
- 1 clove garlic, minced
- 1 tbsp chopped parsley

Directions:

1. Preheat air fryer to 190°C/375°F.
2. Coat the parsnips and carrots with some olive oil and salt.
3. Place them in the frying basket and Air Fry for 10 minutes, tossing once.
4. In a bowl, whisk tahini, lemon juice, 1 tsp of water, and

garlic.
5. Pour the sauce over the cooked veggies.
6. Scatter with parsley and serve.

Variations & Ingredients Tips:

- Add diced potatoes or sweet potatoes to the mix.
- Use Greek yogurt instead of tahini for the sauce.
- Sprinkle with za'atar or dukkah spice blend.

Per Serving: Calories: 80; Total Fat: 4g; Saturated Fat: 0g; Cholesterol: 0mg; Sodium: 260mg; Total Carbs: 10g; Fiber: 3g; Sugars: 3g; Protein: 2g

Mini Hasselback Potatoes

Cooking Time: 25 Minutes | Prep Time: 10 Minutes | Servings: 4

Ingredients:

- 680g baby Yukon gold potatoes (about 10)
- 5 tablespoons butter, cut into very thin slices
- Salt and freshly ground black pepper
- 1 tablespoon vegetable oil
- 1/4 cup grated Parmesan cheese (optional)
- Chopped fresh parsley or chives

Directions:

1. Preheat the air fryer to 200°C/400°F.
2. Make 6-8 deep vertical slits across the top of each potato about 3/4 of the way down.
3. Place a thin butter slice between each of the slices and season generously with salt and pepper.
4. Transfer potatoes to the air fryer basket, packing them in tightly. Some may sit on top of others.
5. Air fry for 20 minutes.
6. Spray or brush potatoes with vegetable oil and sprinkle with Parmesan cheese.
7. Air fry for an additional 5 minutes.
8. Garnish with chopped parsley or chives and serve hot.

Variations & Ingredients Tips:

- Use sweet potatoes instead of Yukon golds.
- Mix shredded cheese into the butter before slicing.
- Brush with garlic butter after cooking.

Per Serving: Calories: 221; Total Fat: 11g; Saturated Fat: 6g; Cholesterol: 24mg; Sodium: 147mg; Total Carbohydrates: 28g; Dietary Fiber: 3g; Total Sugars: 2g; Protein: 4g

Florentine Stuffed Tomatoes

Servings: 2 | Prep Time: 10 Minutes | Cooking Time: 12 Minutes

Ingredients:

- 1 cup frozen spinach, thawed and squeezed dry
- 1/4 cup toasted pine nuts
- 1/4 cup grated mozzarella cheese
- 1/2 cup crumbled feta cheese
- 1/2 cup coarse fresh breadcrumbs
- 1 tablespoon olive oil
- Salt and freshly ground black pepper
- 2 to 3 beefsteak tomatoes, halved horizontally and insides scooped out

Directions:

1. Combine spinach, pine nuts, mozzarella, feta, breadcrumbs, olive oil, salt and pepper in a bowl.
2. Spoon the mixture into the tomato halves, enough for 2-3 tomatoes.
3. Preheat air fryer to 177°C/350°F.
4. Place 3-4 stuffed tomato halves in the air fryer basket and cook for 12 mins until tops are lightly browned.
5. Let cool 1-2 mins before serving.

Variations & Ingredients Tips:

- Use panko breadcrumbs instead of fresh.
- Substitute parmesan for the feta cheese.
- Add minced garlic or lemon zest to the filling.

Per Serving: Calories: 390; Total Fat: 24g; Saturated Fat: 7g; Cholesterol: 35mg; Sodium: 790mg; Total Carbs: 32g; Fiber: 6g; Sugars: 9g; Protein: 17g

Simple Peppared Carrot Chips

Servings: 4 | Prep Time: 5 Minutes | Cooking Time: 15 Minutes

Ingredients:

- 3 carrots, cut into coins
- 1 tablespoon sesame oil
- Salt and pepper to taste

Directions:

1. Preheat air fryer at 190°C/375°F.
2. Combine all ingredients in a bowl.
3. Place carrots in the frying basket and Roast for 10 minutes, tossing once.
4. Serve right away.

Variations & Ingredients Tips:

- Try using different types of seasoning, such as garlic powder, cumin, or smoked paprika for a unique flavor.
- For a sweeter version, toss the carrots with a little honey or maple syrup before cooking.
- Serve the carrot chips with a dipping sauce, such as hummus or ranch dressing.

Per Serving: Calories: 60; Total Fat: 4g; Saturated Fat: 0.5g; Cholesterol: 0mg; Sodium: 135mg; Total Carbs: 6g; Fiber: 2g; Sugars: 3g; Protein: 1g

Sweet Potato Curly Fries

Servings: 4 | Prep Time: 10 Minutes | Cooking Time: 10 Minutes

Ingredients:

- 2 medium sweet potatoes, washed
- 2 tablespoons avocado oil
- ¾ teaspoon salt, divided
- 1 medium avocado
- ½ teaspoon garlic pow-
- der
- ½ teaspoon paprika
- ¼ teaspoon black pepper
- ½ juice lime
- 3 tablespoons fresh cilantro

Directions:

1. Preheat the air fryer to 200°C/400°F.
2. Using a spiralizer, create curly spirals with the sweet potatoes. Keep the pieces about 4 cm long. Continue until all the potatoes are used.
3. In a large bowl, toss the curly sweet potatoes with the avocado oil and ½ teaspoon of the salt.
4. Place the potatoes in the air fryer basket and cook for 5 minutes; shake and cook another 5 minutes.
5. While cooking, add the avocado, garlic, paprika, pepper, the remaining ¼ teaspoon of salt, lime juice, and cilantro to a blender and process until smooth. Set aside.
6. When cooking completes, remove the fries and serve warm with the lime avocado sauce.

Variations & Ingredients Tips:

- Use different types of potatoes, such as russet or Yukon Gold, for a variety of flavors and textures.
- Add some chili powder or cayenne pepper to the spice mixture for a spicy kick.
- Serve the fries with different dipping sauces, such as ranch dressing or ketchup.

Per Serving: Calories: 200; Total Fat: 12g; Saturated Fat: 2g; Cholesterol: 0mg; Sodium: 440mg; Total Carbs: 23g; Fiber: 5g; Sugars: 5g; Protein: 2g

Brown Rice And Goat Cheese Croquettes

Servings: 3 | Prep Time: 15 Minutes | Cooking Time: 8 Minutes

Ingredients:

- ¾ cup Water
- 6 tablespoons Raw medium-grain brown rice, such as brown Arborio
- ½ cup Shredded carrot
- ¼ cup Walnut pieces
- 3 tablespoons (about 43g) Soft goat cheese
- 1 tablespoon Pasteurized egg substitute, such as Egg Beaters (gluten-free, if a concern)
- ¼ teaspoon Dried thyme
- ¼ teaspoon Table salt
- ¼ teaspoon Ground
- black pepper
- Olive oil spray

Directions:

1. Combine the water, rice, and carrots in a small saucepan set over medium-high heat. Bring to a boil, stirring occasionally. Cover, reduce the heat to very low, and simmer very slowly for 45 minutes, or until the water has been absorbed and the rice is tender. Set aside, covered, for 10 minutes.
2. Scrape the contents of the saucepan into a food processor. Cool for 10 minutes.
3. Preheat the air fryer to 200°C/400°F.
4. Put the nuts, cheese, egg substitute, thyme, salt, and pepper into the food processor. Cover and pulse to a coarse paste, stopping the machine at least once to scrape down the inside of the canister.
5. Uncover the food processor; scrape down and remove the blade. Using wet, clean hands, form the mixture into two 10cm-diameter patties for a small batch, three 10cm-diameter patties for a medium batch, or four 10cm-diameter patties for a large one. Generously coat both sides of the patties with olive oil spray.
6. Set the patties in the basket with as much air space between them as possible. Air-fry undisturbed for 8 minutes, or until brown and crisp.
7. Use a nonstick-safe spatula to transfer the croquettes to a wire rack. Cool for 5 minutes before serving.

Variations & Ingredients Tips:

- Substitute different grains like quinoa or farro for the brown rice.
- Add finely chopped spinach or kale to the mixture.
- Serve with a yogurt dill sauce for dipping.

Per Serving: Calories: 225; Total Fat: 10g; Saturated Fat: 3g; Cholesterol: 5mg; Sodium: 330mg; Total Carbs: 27g; Fiber: 3g; Sugars: 2g; Protein: 8g

Veggie Fritters

Servings: 4 | Prep Time: 15 Minutes | Cooking Time: 35 Minutes

Ingredients:

- ¼ cup crumbled feta cheese
- 1 grated zucchini
- ¼ cup Parmesan cheese
- 2 tbsp minced onion
- 1 tbsp garlic powder
- 1 tbsp flour
- 1 tbsp cornmeal
- 1 tbsp butter, melted
- 1 egg
- 2 tsp chopped dill
- 2 tsp chopped parsley
- Salt and pepper to taste
- 1 cup bread crumbs

Directions:

1. Preheat air fryer at 175°C/350°F. Squeeze grated zucchini between paper towels to remove excess moisture. In a

bowl, combine all ingredients except breadcrumbs. Form mixture into 12 balls, about 2 tbsp each. In a shallow bowl, add breadcrumbs. Roll each ball in breadcrumbs, covering all sides. Place fritters on an ungreased pizza pan. Place in the frying basket and air fry for 11 minutes, flipping once. Serve.

Variations & Ingredients Tips:

- Add grated carrots, sweet potatoes, or beets for a colorful twist.
- Use goat cheese, ricotta, or mozzarella instead of feta for a different flavor profile.
- Serve with tzatziki sauce, marinara sauce, or ranch dressing for dipping.

Per Serving: Calories: 264; Total Fat: 14g; Saturated Fat: 7g; Cholesterol: 74mg; Sodium: 566mg; Total Carbohydrates: 25g; Dietary Fiber: 2g; Total Sugars: 3g; Protein: 11g

Buttered Brussels Sprouts

Servings: 4 | Prep Time: 5 Minutes | Cooking Time: 30 Minutes

Ingredients:

- ¼ cup grated Parmesan
- 2 tbsp butter, melted
- 455g Brussels sprouts
- Salt and pepper to taste

Directions:

1. Preheat air fryer to 165°C/330°F.
2. Trim the bottoms of the sprouts and remove any discolored leaves.
3. Place the sprouts in a medium bowl along with butter, salt and pepper. Toss to coat, then place them in the frying basket.
4. Roast for 20 minutes, shaking the basket twice. When done, the sprouts should be crisp with golden-brown color.
5. Plate the sprouts in a serving dish and toss with Parmesan cheese.

Variations & Ingredients Tips:

- Add crushed garlic or garlic powder to the butter mixture.
- Toss with balsamic glaze or lemon juice after cooking.
- Use olive oil instead of butter to make it vegan.

Per Serving: Calories: 130; Total Fat: 8g; Saturated Fat: 4g; Cholesterol: 15mg; Sodium: 230mg; Total Carbs: 11g; Fiber: 4g; Sugars: 3g; Protein: 6g

Caraway Seed Pretzel Sticks

Servings: 4 | Prep Time: 10 Minutes | Cooking Time: 30 Minutes

Ingredients:

- ½ pizza dough
- 1 tsp baking soda
- 2 tbsp caraway seeds

Directions:

1. Preheat air fryer to 200°C/400°F.
2. Roll out the dough, on parchment paper, into a rectangle, then cut it into 8 strips.
3. Whisk the baking soda and 1 cup of hot water until well dissolved in a bowl. Submerge each strip, shake off any excess, and stretch another 2.5-5cm.
4. Scatter with caraway seeds and let rise for 10 minutes in the frying basket.
5. Grease with cooking spray and Air Fry for 8 minutes until golden brown, turning once.
6. Serve.

Variations & Ingredients Tips:

- Use store-bought pizza dough or make your own from scratch.
- Add grated parmesan or coarse salt to the topping.
- Serve with mustard or beer cheese dip.

Per Serving: Calories: 120; Total Fat: 2g; Saturated Fat: 0g; Cholesterol: 0mg; Sodium: 200mg; Total Carbs: 22g; Fiber: 1g; Sugars: 1g; Protein: 3g

Baked Shishito Peppers

Servings: 2 | Prep Time: 5 Minutes | Cooking Time: 15 Minutes

Ingredients:

- 170g shishito peppers
- 1 tsp olive oil
- 1 tsp salt
- ¼ cup soy sauce

Directions:

1. Preheat air fryer at 190°C/375°F.
2. Combine all ingredients in a bowl.
3. Place peppers in the frying basket and Bake for 8 minutes until the peppers are blistered, shaking once.
4. Serve with soy sauce for dipping.

Variations & Ingredients Tips:

- Toss with lemon juice and parmesan after baking.
- Sprinkle with togarashi or chili powder for extra heat.
- Substitute ponzu sauce for the soy sauce.

Per Serving: Calories: 52; Total Fat: 3g; Saturated Fat: 0g; Cholesterol: 0mg; Sodium: 1225mg; Total Carbs: 6g; Fiber: 2g; Sugars: 3g; Protein: 2g

Southern Okra Chips

Servings: 2 | Prep Time: 10 Minutes | Cooking

Ingredients:

- 2 eggs
- 60 ml whole milk
- 60 ml bread crumbs
- 60 ml cornmeal
- 1 tablespoon Cajun seasoning
- Salt and pepper to taste
- ⅛ teaspoon chili pepper
- 225 g okra, sliced
- 1 tablespoon butter, melted

Directions:

1. Preheat air fryer at 200°C/400°F.
2. Beat the eggs and milk in a bowl.
3. In another bowl, combine the remaining ingredients, except okra and butter.
4. Dip okra chips in the egg mixture, then dredge them in the breadcrumbs mixture.
5. Place okra chips in the greased frying basket and Roast for 7 minutes, shake once and brush with melted butter.
6. Serve right away.

Variations & Ingredients Tips:

- Use panko breadcrumbs or crushed crackers instead of regular breadcrumbs for a crunchier texture.
- Add some grated Parmesan cheese or nutritional yeast to the breadcrumb mixture for a cheesy flavor.
- Serve the okra chips with a dipping sauce, such as ranch dressing or remoulade sauce.

Per Serving: Calories: 320; Total Fat: 16g; Saturated Fat: 6g; Cholesterol: 205mg; Sodium: 840mg; Total Carbs: 33g; Fiber: 4g; Sugars: 5g; Protein: 13g

Home Fries

Servings: 4 | Prep Time: 10 Minutes | Cooking Time: 20 Minutes

Ingredients:

- 1.4kg potatoes, cut into 2.5cm cubes
- 1/2 teaspoon oil
- Salt and pepper

Directions:

1. In a large bowl, mix the potatoes and oil thoroughly.
2. Cook at 200°C/390°F for 10 minutes and shake the basket to redistribute potatoes.
3. Cook for an additional 10 minutes, until brown and crisp.
4. Season with salt and pepper to taste.

Variations & Ingredients Tips:

- Add paprika, garlic powder or other spices to the potatoes.
- Mix in diced onions or bell peppers.
- Toss with parsley or chives after cooking.

Per Serving: Calories: 288; Total Fat: 1g; Saturated Fat: 0g; Cholesterol: 0mg; Sodium: 15mg; Total Carbs: 63g; Dietary Fiber: 5g; Total Sugars: 2g; Protein: 6g

Sweet Potato Puffs

Servings: 18 | Prep Time: 20 Minutes | Cooking Time: 35 Minutes

Ingredients:

- 3 sweet potatoes (225 to 280 g each)
- 1 cup seasoned Italian-style dried bread crumbs
- 3 tablespoons all-purpose flour
- 3 tablespoons instant mashed potato flakes
- ¾ teaspoon onion powder
- ¾ teaspoon table salt
- Olive oil spray

Directions:

1. Preheat the air fryer to 180°C/350°F.
2. Prick the sweet potatoes in four or five different places with the tines of a flatware fork (not in a line but all around the sweet potatoes).
3. When the machine is at temperature, set the sweet potatoes in the basket with as much air space between them as possible. Air-fry undisturbed for 20 minutes.
4. Use kitchen tongs to transfer the sweet potatoes to a wire rack. (They will still be firm; they are only partially cooked.) Cool for 10 to 15 minutes. Meanwhile, increase the machine's temperature to 200°C/400°F. Spread the bread crumbs on a dinner plate.
5. Peel the sweet potatoes. Shred them through the large holes of a box grater into a large bowl. Stir in the flour, potato flakes, onion powder, and salt until well combined.
6. Scoop up 2 tablespoons of the sweet potato mixture. Form it into a small puff, a cylinder about like a Tater Tot. Set this cylinder in the bread crumbs. Gently roll it around to coat on all sides, even the ends. Set aside on a cutting board and continue making more puffs: 11 more for a small batch, 17 more for a medium batch, or 23 more for a large batch.
7. Generously coat the puffs with olive oil spray on all sides. Set the puffs in the basket with as much air space between them as possible. They should not be touching, but even a fraction of an cm will work well. Air-fry undisturbed for 15 minutes, or until lightly browned and crunchy.
8. Gently turn the contents of the basket out onto a wire rack. Cool the puffs for a couple of minutes before serving.

Variations & Ingredients Tips:

- Use different types of breadcrumbs, such as panko or cornmeal, for a variety of textures.
- Add some chopped fresh herbs, such as parsley or chives, to the sweet potato mixture for extra flavor.
- Serve the puffs with a dipping sauce, such as honey mustard or sweet chili sauce.

Per Serving: Calories: 70; Total Fat: 1g; Saturated Fat: 0g; Cholesterol: 0mg; Sodium: 150mg; Total Carbs: 13g; Fiber: 1g; Sugars: 2g; Protein: 1g

Chicken Eggrolls

Servings: 10 Eggrolls | Prep Time: 20 Minutes | Cooking Time: 17 Minutes

Ingredients:

- 1 tablespoon vegetable oil
- ¼ cup chopped onion
- 1 clove garlic, minced
- 1 cup shredded carrot
- ½ cup thinly sliced celery
- 2 cups cooked chicken
- 2 cups shredded white cabbage
- ½ cup teriyaki sauce
- 20 egg roll wrappers
- 1 egg, whisked
- 1 tablespoon water

Directions:

1. Preheat the air fryer to 200°C/390°F.
2. In a skillet, heat the oil over medium-high heat. Add onion and sauté for 1 min. Add garlic and sauté 30 secs.
3. Add carrot, celery and cook 2 mins. Add chicken, cabbage, teriyaki sauce. Cook 1 min, stirring.
4. In a bowl, whisk egg and water for brushing wrappers.
5. Lay wrappers at an angle. Place ¼ cup filling in center. Fold bottom corner up, fold in sides, roll up.
6. Place eggrolls in air fryer basket, spray with cooking spray. Cook 8 mins, turn and cook 2-4 mins more.

Variations & Ingredients Tips:

- Use pork or shrimp instead of chicken.
- Omit teriyaki sauce and use soy sauce & rice vinegar instead.
- Add shredded cabbage or bean sprouts to filling.

Per Serving: Calories: 150; Total Fat: 4g; Saturated Fat: 1g; Cholesterol: 35mg; Sodium: 460mg; Total Carbs: 20g; Fiber: 1g; Sugars: 2g; Protein: 8g

Succulent Roasted Peppers

Servings: 2 | Prep Time: 5 Minutes | Cooking Time: 35 Minutes

Ingredients:

- 2 red bell peppers
- 2 tablespoons olive oil
- Salt to taste
- 1 teaspoon dill, chopped

Directions:

1. Preheat air fryer to 200°C/400°F.
2. Remove the tops and bottoms of the peppers. Cut along rib sections and discard the seeds.
3. Combine the bell peppers and olive oil in a bowl.

4. Place bell peppers in the frying basket. Roast for 24 minutes, flipping once.
5. Transfer the roasted peppers to a small bowl and cover for 15 minutes.
6. Then, peel and discard the skins. Sprinkle with salt and dill and serve.

Variations & Ingredients Tips:

- Use different colors of bell peppers, such as yellow or orange, for a colorful presentation.
- Add some minced garlic or onion for extra flavor.
- Serve the roasted peppers with goat cheese or feta cheese for a creamy and tangy contrast.

Per Serving: Calories: 140; Total Fat: 14g; Saturated Fat: 2g; Cholesterol: 0mg; Sodium: 150mg; Total Carbs: 6g; Fiber: 2g; Sugars: 4g; Protein: 1g

Roasted Herbed Shiitake Mushrooms

Cooking Time: 5 Minutes | Prep Time: 5 Minutes | Servings: 4

Ingredients:

- 227g shiitake mushrooms, stemmed and caps chopped
- 1 tablespoon olive oil
- 1/2 teaspoon salt
- Freshly ground black pepper
- 1 teaspoon chopped fresh thyme
- 1 teaspoon chopped fresh oregano
- 1 tablespoon chopped fresh parsley

Directions:

1. Preheat air fryer to 200°C/400°F.
2. In a bowl, toss mushrooms with olive oil, salt, pepper, thyme and oregano.
3. Transfer mushrooms to air fryer basket and cook for 5 minutes, shaking basket 1-2 times.
4. For more tender mushrooms, increase cook time by 2 minutes.
5. Once cooked, toss mushrooms with chopped parsley.
6. Season again to taste and serve.

Variations & Ingredients Tips:

- Use a blend of wild mushroom varieties.
- Add minced garlic or shallots before roasting.
- Finish with a squeeze of lemon juice.

Per Serving: Calories: 55; Total Fat: 4g; Saturated Fat: 1g; Cholesterol: 0mg; Sodium: 234mg; Total Carbohydrates: 4g; Dietary Fiber: 1g; Total Sugars: 2g; Protein: 2g

Stunning Apples & Onions

Servings: 4 | Prep Time: 5 Minutes | Cooking Time:

Ingredients:

- 2 peeled McIntosh apples, sliced
- 1 shallot, sliced
- 2 teaspoons canola oil
- 2 tablespoons brown

- sugar
- 1 tablespoon honey
- 1 tablespoon butter, melted
- ½ teaspoon sea salt

Directions:

1. Preheat the air fryer to 165°C/325°F.
2. Toss the shallot slices with oil in a bowl until coated. Put the bowl in the fryer and Bake for 5 minutes.
3. Remove the bowl and add the apples, brown sugar, honey, melted butter, and sea salt and stir.
4. Put the bowl back into the fryer and Bake for 10-12 more minutes or until the onions and apples are tender.
5. Stir again and serve.

Variations & Ingredients Tips:

- Use different types of apples, such as Granny Smith or Honeycrisp, for a variety of flavors and textures.
- Add some chopped nuts, such as pecans or walnuts, for a crunchy texture.
- For a savory version, replace the brown sugar and honey with balsamic vinegar and thyme.

Per Serving: Calories: 140; Total Fat: 5g; Saturated Fat: 2g; Cholesterol: 10mg; Sodium: 300mg; Total Carbs: 25g; Fiber: 2g; Sugars: 20g; Protein: 0g

Cheesy Texas Toast

Servings: 2 | Prep Time: 5 Minutes | Cooking Time: 4 Minutes

Ingredients:

- 2 2.5cm-thick slices Italian bread (each about 10cm across)
- 4 teaspoons Softened butter

- 2 teaspoons Minced garlic
- ¼ cup (about 21g) Finely grated Parmesan cheese

Directions:

1. Preheat the air fryer to 200°C/400°F.
2. Spread one side of each bread slice with 2 tsp butter. Sprinkle with 1 tsp minced garlic, followed by 2 tbsp grated cheese.
3. When the machine is at temperature, put the bread slices cheese side up in the basket with space between them.
4. Air-fry undisturbed for 4 minutes, or until browned and crunchy.
5. Use a nonstick-safe spatula to transfer the toasts cheese side up to a wire rack. Cool for 5 minutes before serving.

Variations & Ingredients Tips:

- Add dried Italian seasoning or crushed red pepper to the butter.
- Use different cheese varieties like cheddar, provolone or asiago.
- Brush with garlic butter instead of plain butter.

Per Serving: Calories: 320; Total Fat: 18g; Saturated Fat: 9g; Cholesterol: 35mg; Sodium: 820mg; Total Carbs: 30g; Fiber: 1g; Sugars: 1g; Protein: 10g

Vegetarian Recipes

Black Bean Empanadas

Servings: 12 | Prep Time: 30 Minutes | Cooking Time: 35 Minutes

Ingredients:

- 1½ cups all-purpose flour
- 1 cup whole-wheat flour
- 1 teaspoon salt
- ½ cup cold unsalted butter
- 1 egg
- ½ cup milk
- One 400-g can black beans, drained and rinsed
- ¼ cup chopped cilantro
- 1 cup shredded purple cabbage
- 1 cup shredded Monterey jack cheese
- ¼ cup salsa

Directions:

1. In a food processor, place the all-purpose flour, whole-wheat flour, salt, and butter into processor and process for 2 minutes, scraping down the sides of the food processor every 30 seconds. Add in the egg and blend for 30 seconds. Using the pulse button, add in the milk 1 tablespoon at a time, or until dough is moist enough to handle and be rolled into a ball. Let the dough rest at room temperature for 30 minutes.
2. Meanwhile, in a large bowl, mix together the black beans, cilantro, cabbage, Monterey Jack cheese, and salsa.
3. On a floured surface, cut the dough in half; then form a ball and cut each ball into 6 equal pieces, totaling 12 equal pieces. Work with one piece at a time, and cover the remaining dough with a towel.
4. Roll out a piece of dough into a 15-cm round, much like a tortilla, 6-mm thick. Place 4 tablespoons of filling in the center of the round, and fold over to form a half-circle. Using a fork, crimp the edges together and pierce the top for air holes. Repeat with the remaining dough and filling.
5. Preheat the air fryer to 175°C/350°F.
6. Working in batches, place 3 to 4 empanadas in the air fryer basket and spray with cooking spray. Cook for 4 minutes, flip over the empanadas and spray with cooking spray, and cook another 4 minutes.

Variations & Ingredients Tips:

- Use store-bought empanada dough or puff pastry for a quicker version.
- Substitute black beans with shredded chicken or ground beef for a non-vegetarian option.
- Serve with guacamole, sour cream, or hot sauce for dipping.

Per Serving (1 empanada): Calories: 220; Cholesterol: 35mg; Total Fat: 11g; Saturated Fat: 6g; Sodium: 300mg; Total Carbohydrates: 25g; Dietary Fiber: 3g; Total Sugars: 2g; Protein: 8g

Spinach And Cheese Calzone

Servings: 2 | Prep Time: 20 Minutes | Cooking Time: 10 Minutes

Ingredients:

- ⅔ cup frozen chopped spinach, thawed
- 1 cup grated mozzarella cheese
- 1 cup ricotta cheese
- ½ teaspoon Italian seasoning
- ½ teaspoon salt
- freshly ground black pepper
- 1 store-bought or homemade pizza dough* (about 340 to 454 grams)
- 2 tablespoons olive oil
- pizza or marinara sauce (optional)

Directions:

1. Drain and squeeze all the water out of the thawed spinach and set it aside. Mix the mozzarella cheese, ricotta cheese, Italian seasoning, salt and freshly ground black pepper together in a bowl. Stir in the chopped spinach.
2. Divide the dough in half. With floured hands or on a floured surface, stretch or roll one half of the dough into a 25-cm circle. Spread half of the cheese and spinach mixture on half of the dough, leaving about 5 cm of dough empty around the edge.
3. Fold the other half of the dough over the cheese mixture, almost to the edge of the bottom dough to form a half moon. Fold the bottom edge of dough up over the top edge and crimp the dough around the edges in order to make the crust and seal the calzone. Brush the dough with olive oil. Repeat with the second half of dough to make the second calzone.
4. Preheat the air fryer to 180°C/360°F.
5. Brush or spray the air fryer basket with olive oil. Air-fry the calzones one at a time for 10 minutes, flipping the calzone over half way through. Serve with warm pizza or marinara sauce if desired.

Variations & Ingredients Tips:

- Add sautéed mushrooms, onions, or bell peppers to the filling.
- Use a combination of different cheeses like feta, provolone, or Parmesan.
- Brush the calzone with garlic butter or sprinkle with Italian seasoning before air frying.

Per Serving: Calories: 790; Total Fat: 41g; Saturated Fat: 19g; Sodium: 1480mg; Total Carbohydrates: 70g; Dietary Fiber: 4g; Total Sugars: 4g; Protein: 38g

Parmesan Portobello Mushroom Caps

Servings: 2 | Prep Time: 10 Minutes | Cooking Time: 14 Minutes

Ingredients:

- ¼ cup flour
- 1 egg, lightly beaten
- 1 cup seasoned bread-crumbs*
- 2 large portobello mush-room caps, stems and gills removed
- olive oil, in a spray bot-tle
- ½ cup tomato sauce
- ¾ cup grated mozzarella cheese
- 1 tablespoon grated Parmesan cheese
- 1 tablespoon chopped fresh basil or parsley

Directions:

1. Set up a dredging station with three shallow dishes. Place the flour in the first shallow dish, egg in the second dish and breadcrumbs in the last dish.
2. Dredge the mushrooms in flour, then dip them into the egg and finally press them into the breadcrumbs to coat on all sides. Spray both sides of the coated mushrooms with olive oil.
3. Preheat the air fryer to 200°C/400°F.
4. Air-fry the mushrooms at 200°C/400°F for 10 minutes, turning them over halfway through the cooking process.
5. Fill the underside of the mushrooms with the tomato sauce and then top the sauce with the mozzarella and Parmesan cheeses.
6. Reset the air fryer temperature to 180°C/350°F and air-fry for an additional 4 minutes, until the cheese has melted and is slightly browned.
7. Serve the mushrooms with pasta tossed with tomato sauce and garnish with some chopped fresh basil or parsley.

Variations & Ingredients Tips:

- Use panko breadcrumbs for a crispier texture.
- Add Italian seasoning or garlic powder to the breadcrumbs for extra flavor.
- Substitute tomato sauce with pesto or Alfredo sauce.

Per Serving: Calories: 330; Total Fat: 16g; Saturated Fat: 7g; Sodium: 960mg; Total Carbohydrates: 28g; Dietary Fiber: 3g; Total Sugars: 6g; Protein: 22g

Vegan Buddha Bowls

Servings: 2 | Prep Time: 20 Minutes | Cooking Time: 45 Minutes

Ingredients:

- 1/2 cup quinoa
- 1 cup sweet potato cubes
- 340 grams broccoli florets
- 3/4 cup bread crumbs
- 1/4 cup chickpea flour
- 1/4 cup hot sauce
- 454 grams super-firm tofu, cubed
- 1 tsp lemon juice
- 2 tsp olive oil
- Salt to taste
- 2 scallions, thinly sliced
- 1 tbsp sesame seeds

Directions:

1. Preheat air fryer to 200°C/400°F.
2. Add quinoa and 1 cup of boiling water in a baking pan, cover it with aluminum foil, and Air Fry for 10 minutes. Set aside covered.
3. Put the sweet potatoes in the air fryer basket and Air Fry for 2 minutes. Add in broccoli and Air Fry for 5 more minutes. Shake up and cook for another 3 minutes. Set the veggies aside.
4. On a plate, put the breadcrumbs. In a bowl, whisk chickpea flour and hot sauce. Toss in tofu cubes until coated and dip them in the breadcrumbs.
5. Air Fry tofu for 10 minutes until crispy.
6. Share quinoa and fried veggies into 2 bowls. Top with crispy tofu and drizzle with lemon juice, olive oil and salt to taste.
7. Scatter with scallions and sesame seeds before serving.

Variations & Ingredients Tips:

- Use cauliflower, Brussels sprouts, or carrots instead of broccoli.
- Substitute quinoa with brown rice, farro, or couscous.
- Add avocado slices or hummus for extra creaminess.

Per Serving: Calories: 620; Total Fat: 26g; Saturated Fat: 3.5g; Sodium: 1120mg; Total Carbohydrates: 71g; Dietary Fiber: 11g; Total Sugars: 9g; Protein: 35g

Golden Breaded Mushrooms

Servings: 2 | Prep Time: 15 Minutes | Cooking Time: 20 Minutes

Ingredients:

- 2 cups crispy rice cereal
- 1 tsp nutritional yeast
- 2 tsp garlic powder
- 1 tsp dried oregano
- 1 tsp dried basil
- Salt to taste
- 1 tbsp Dijon mustard
- 1 tbsp mayonnaise
- 1/4 cup milk
- 225g whole mushrooms
- 4 tbsp chili sauce
- 3 tbsp mayonnaise

Directions:

1. Preheat air fryer at 175°C/350°F.
2. Blend rice cereal, garlic powder, oregano, basil, nutritional yeast, and salt in a food processor until it gets a bread-crumb consistency. Set aside in a bowl.
3. Mix the mustard, 1 tbsp mayonnaise, and milk in a bowl. Dip mushrooms in the mustard mixture; shake off excess.

Then, dredge them in the breadcrumbs; shake off excess.
4. Place mushrooms in the greased frying basket and Air Fry for 7 minutes, shaking once.
5. Mix the 3 tbsp mayonnaise with chili sauce in a small bowl. Serve the mushrooms with the dipping sauce on the side.

Variations & Ingredients Tips:

● Use panko breadcrumbs instead of rice cereal for extra crunch.
● Add paprika or cayenne to the breading for a kick of spice.
● Stuff the mushroom caps with cheese or pesto before breading.

Per Serving: Calories: 340; Total Fat: 20g; Saturated Fat: 3g; Sodium: 900mg; Total Carbs: 35g; Dietary Fiber: 3g; Total Sugars: 6g; Protein: 7g

Tacos

Servings: 24 | Prep Time: 20 Minutes | Cooking Time: 8 Minutes Per Batch

Ingredients:

● 1 24-count package 10-cm corn tortillas
● 1½ cups refried beans (about ¾ of a 425-gram can)
● 113 grams sharp Cheddar cheese, grated
● ½ cup salsa
● oil for misting or cooking spray

Directions:

1. Preheat air fryer to 200°C/390°F.
2. Wrap refrigerated tortillas in damp paper towels and microwave for 30 to 60 seconds to warm. If necessary, rewarm tortillas as you go to keep them soft enough to fold without breaking.
3. Working with one tortilla at a time, top with 1 tablespoon of beans, 1 tablespoon of grated cheese, and 1 teaspoon of salsa. Fold over and press down very gently on the center. Press edges firmly all around to seal. Spray both sides with oil or cooking spray.
4. Cooking in two batches, place half the tacos in the air fryer basket. To cook 12 at a time, you may need to stand them upright and lean some against the sides of basket. It's okay if they're crowded as long as you leave a little room for air to circulate around them.
5. Cook for 8 minutes or until golden brown and crispy.
6. Repeat steps 4 and 5 to cook remaining tacos.

Variations & Ingredients Tips:

● Use black beans, pinto beans, or vegetarian chili instead of refried beans.
● Add diced avocado, shredded lettuce, or chopped tomatoes as additional fillings.
● Serve with guacamole, sour cream, or hot sauce on the

side.

Per Serving: Calories: 80; Total Fat: 3g; Saturated Fat: 1.5g; Sodium: 180mg; Total Carbohydrates: 10g; Dietary Fiber: 2g; Total Sugars: 1g; Protein: 3g

Party Giant Nachos

Servings: 2 | Prep Time: 10 Minutes | Cooking Time: 20 Minutes

Ingredients:

● 2 tbsp sour cream
● ½ tsp chili powder
● Salt to taste
● 2 soft corn tortillas
● 2 tsp avocado oil
● ½ cup refried beans
● ¼ cup cheddar cheese shreds
● 2 tbsp Parmesan cheese
● 2 tbsp sliced black olives
● ¼ cup torn iceberg lettuce
● ¼ cup baby spinach
● ½ sliced avocado
● 1 tomato, diced
● 2 lime wedges

Directions:

1. Preheat air fryer at 200°C/400°F.
2. Whisk the sour cream, chili powder, and salt in a small bowl.
3. Brush tortillas with avocado oil and season one side with salt. Place tortillas in the air fryer basket and Bake for 3 minutes. Set aside.
4. Layer the refried beans, Parmesan and cheddar cheeses in the tortillas. Place them back into the basket and Bake for 2 minutes.
5. Divide tortillas into 2 serving plates. Top each tortilla with black olives, baby spinach, lettuce, and tomatoes. Dollop sour cream mixture on each.
6. Serve with lime and avocado wedges on the side.

Variations & Ingredients Tips:

● Add sliced jalapeños or hot sauce for a spicy kick.
● Use Greek yogurt instead of sour cream for a healthier option.
● Substitute refried beans with black beans or pinto beans.

Per Serving: Calories: 380; Total Fat: 24g; Saturated Fat: 7g; Sodium: 780mg; Total Carbohydrates: 32g; Dietary Fiber: 9g; Total Sugars: 5g; Protein: 13g

Quinoa Green Pizza

Servings: 2 | Prep Time: 10 Minutes | Cooking Time: 25 Minutes

Ingredients:

● ¾ cup quinoa flour
● ½ tsp dried basil
● ½ tsp dried oregano
● 1 tbsp apple cider vinegar
● 1/3 cup ricotta cheese

| 2/3 cup chopped broccoli | ½ tsp garlic powder |

Directions:

1. Preheat air fryer to 180°C/350°F.
2. Whisk quinoa flour, basil, oregano, apple cider vinegar, and ½ cup of water until smooth. Set aside.
3. Cut 2 pieces of parchment paper. Place the quinoa mixture on one paper, top with another piece, and flatten to create a crust. Discard the top piece of paper.
4. Bake for 5 minutes, turn and discard the other piece of paper.
5. Spread the ricotta cheese over the crust, scatter with broccoli, and sprinkle with garlic.
6. Grill at 200°C/400°F for 5 minutes until golden brown. Serve warm.

Variations & Ingredients Tips:

- Add sliced mushrooms, bell peppers, or onions as additional toppings.
- Use pesto or tomato sauce instead of ricotta for a different flavor.
- Sprinkle with red pepper flakes for some heat.

Per Serving: Calories: 310; Total Fat: 9g; Saturated Fat: 4g; Sodium: 160mg; Total Carbohydrates: 45g; Dietary Fiber: 5g; Total Sugars: 2g; Protein: 13g

Bite-sized Blooming Onions

Servings: 4 | Prep Time: 20 Minutes | Cooking Time: 35 Minutes + Cooling Time

Ingredients:

450 grams cipollini onions	½ tsp paprika
1 cup flour	1 tsp cayenne pepper
1 tsp salt	2 eggs
	2 tbsp milk

Directions:

1. Preheat the air fryer to 190°C/375°F. Carefully peel the onions and cut a 25-cm off the stem ends and trim the root ends. Place them root-side down on the cutting surface and cut the onions into quarters. Be careful not to cut all the way to the bottom. Cut each quarter into 2 sections and pull the wedges apart without breaking them.
2. In a shallow bowl, add the flour, salt, paprika, and cayenne, and in a separate shallow bowl, beat the eggs with the milk. Dip the onions in the flour, then dip in the egg mix, coating evenly, and then in the flour mix again. Shake off excess flour. Put the onions in the frying basket, cut-side up, and spray with cooking oil. Air Fry for 10-15 minutes until the onions are crispy on the outside, tender on the inside. Let cool for 10 minutes, then serve.

Variations & Ingredients Tips:

- Serve with ranch or blue cheese dressing for dipping.
- Use regular yellow onions cut into wedges for a larger version.
- Experiment with different spices like garlic powder, smoked paprika, or cumin in the flour mixture.

Per Serving: Calories: 270; Cholesterol: 95mg; Total Fat: 5g; Saturated Fat: 1g; Sodium: 680mg; Total Carbohydrates: 47g; Dietary Fiber: 3g; Total Sugars: 4g; Protein: 9g

Black Bean Stuffed Potato Boats

Servings: 4 | Prep Time: 15 Minutes | Cooking Time: 55 Minutes

Ingredients:

4 russets potatoes	2 tomatoes, chopped
1 cup chipotle mayonnaise	1 scallion, chopped
1 cup canned black beans	1/3 cup chopped cilantro
	1 poblano chile, minced
	1 avocado, diced

Directions:

1. Preheat air fryer to 200°C/390°F. Clean the potatoes, poke with a fork, and spray with oil. Put in the air fryer and Bake for 30 minutes or until softened.
2. Heat the beans in a pan over medium heat. Put the potatoes on a plate and cut them across the top. Open them with a fork so you can stuff them. Top each potato with chipotle mayonnaise, beans, tomatoes, scallions, cilantro, poblano chile, and avocado. Serve immediately.

Variations & Ingredients Tips:

- Substitute black beans with refried beans or lentils for a different protein option.
- Use sour cream or Greek yogurt instead of chipotle mayonnaise for a milder flavor.
- Add shredded cheese, salsa, or pickled jalapeños for extra toppings.

Per Serving (1 potato): Calories: 490; Cholesterol: 15mg; Total Fat: 33g; Saturated Fat: 5g; Sodium: 670mg; Total Carbohydrates: 46g; Dietary Fiber: 9g; Total Sugars: 6g; Protein: 9g

Garlicky Brussel Sprouts With Saffron Aioli

Servings: 4 | Prep Time: 10 Minutes | Cooking Time: 20 Minutes

Ingredients:

| 455g Brussels sprouts, halved | 1 tsp garlic powder |
| | Salt and pepper to taste |

- 1/2 cup mayonnaise
- 1/2 tbsp olive oil
- 1 tbsp Dijon mustard
- 1 tsp minced garlic
- Salt and pepper to taste
- 1/2 tsp liquid saffron

Directions:

1. Preheat air fryer to 195°C/380°F.
2. Combine the Brussels sprouts, garlic powder, salt and pepper in a large bowl. Place in the fryer and spray with cooking oil.
3. Bake for 12-14 minutes, shaking once, until just browned.
4. Meanwhile, in a small bowl, mix mayonnaise, olive oil, mustard, garlic, saffron, salt and pepper.
5. When the Brussels sprouts are slightly cooled, serve with the saffron aioli.

Variations & Ingredients Tips:

- Add grated parmesan or breadcrumbs over the sprouts before air frying for a crispy topping.
- Substitute Greek yogurt for half the mayo in the aioli.
- Drizzle with balsamic glaze or lemon juice before serving.

Per Serving: Calories: 220; Total Fat: 19g; Saturated Fat: 3g; Sodium: 290mg; Total Carbs: 9g; Dietary Fiber: 3g; Total Sugars: 2g; Protein: 3g

Thyme Meatless Patties

Servings: 3 | Prep Time: 10 Minutes | Cooking Time: 25 Minutes

Ingredients:

- ½ cup oat flour
- 1 tsp allspice
- ½ tsp ground thyme
- 1 tsp maple syrup
- ½ tsp liquid smoke
- 1 tsp balsamic vinegar

Directions:

1. Preheat air fryer to 200°C/400°F.
2. Mix the oat flour, allspice, thyme, maple syrup, liquid smoke, balsamic vinegar, and 2 tbsp of water in a bowl.
3. Make 6 patties out of the mixture. Place them onto a parchment paper and flatten them to 1-cm thick. Grease the patties with cooking spray.
4. Grill for 12 minutes until crispy, turning once.
5. Serve warm.

Variations & Ingredients Tips:

- Add finely chopped walnuts, sunflower seeds, or pumpkin seeds for crunch.
- Use date syrup or agave nectar instead of maple syrup.
- Serve with a dipping sauce like BBQ, ketchup, or sweet chili sauce.

Per Serving: Calories: 110; Total Fat: 2g; Saturated Fat: 0g; Sodium: 5mg; Total Carbohydrates: 19g; Dietary Fiber: 2g; Total Sugars: 4g; Protein: 3g

Fake Shepherd´s Pie

Servings: 6 | Prep Time: 20 Minutes | Cooking Time: 40 Minutes

Ingredients:

- ½ head cauliflower, cut into florets
- 1 sweet potato, diced
- 1 tbsp olive oil
- ¼ cup cheddar shreds
- 2 tbsp milk
- Salt and pepper to taste
- 2 tsp avocado oil
- 1 cup beefless grounds
- ½ onion, diced
- 2 cloves garlic, minced
- 1 carrot, diced
- ½ cup green peas
- 1 stalk celery, diced
- 2/3 cup tomato sauce
- 1 tsp chopped rosemary
- 1 tsp thyme leaves

Directions:

1. Place cauliflower and sweet potato in a pot of salted boiling water over medium heat and simmer for 7 minutes until fork tender. Strain and transfer to a bowl. Put in avocado oil, cheddar, milk, salt and pepper. Mash until smooth.
2. Warm olive oil in a skillet over medium-high heat and stir in beefless grounds and vegetables and stir-fry for 4 minutes until veggies are tender. Stir in tomato sauce, rosemary, thyme, salt, and black pepper. Set aside.
3. Preheat air fryer to 175°C/350°F. Spoon filling into a round cake pan lightly greased with olive oil and cover with the topping. Using the tines of a fork, run shallow lines in the top of cauliflower for a decorative touch. Place cake pan in the frying basket and Air Fry for 12 minutes. Let sit for 10 minutes before serving.

Variations & Ingredients Tips:

- Use mashed potatoes instead of cauliflower and sweet potato for a more traditional topping.
- Substitute beefless grounds with cooked lentils or quinoa for a different protein option.
- Add Worcestershire sauce, soy sauce, or vegetable broth to the filling for extra savory flavor.

Per Serving: Calories: 220; Cholesterol: 10mg; Total Fat: 12g; Saturated Fat: 4g; Sodium: 520mg; Total Carbohydrates: 21g; Dietary Fiber: 5g; Total Sugars: 6g; Protein: 9g

Veggie Fried Rice

Servings: 4 | Prep Time: 10 Minutes | Cooking Time: 25 Minutes

Ingredients:

- 1 cup cooked brown rice
- 1/3 cup chopped onion
- 1/2 cup chopped carrots
- 1/2 cup chopped bell peppers
- 1/2 cup chopped broccoli florets
- 3 tablespoons low-sodium soy sauce
- 1 tablespoon sesame oil

- 1 teaspoon ground ginger
- 1 teaspoon ground garlic powder
- 1/2 teaspoon black pepper
- 1/8 teaspoon salt
- 2 large eggs

Directions:

1. Preheat the air fryer to 190°C/370°F.
2. In a large bowl, mix together the brown rice, onions, carrots, bell pepper, and broccoli.
3. In a small bowl, whisk together the soy sauce, sesame oil, ginger, garlic powder, pepper, salt, and eggs.
4. Pour the egg mixture into the rice and vegetable mixture and mix together.
5. Liberally spray a 18-cm springform pan (or compatible air fryer dish) with olive oil. Add the rice mixture to the pan and cover with aluminum foil.
6. Place a metal trivet into the air fryer basket and set the pan on top. Cook for 15 minutes.
7. Carefully remove the pan from basket, discard the foil, and mix the rice. Return the rice to the air fryer basket, turning down the temperature to 180°C/350°F and cooking another 10 minutes.
8. Remove and let cool 5 minutes. Serve warm.

Variations & Ingredients Tips:

- Add diced tofu or edamame for extra protein.
- Use cauliflower rice for a low-carb option.
- Drizzle with sriracha or chili garlic sauce for heat.

Per Serving: Calories: 253; Total Fat: 8g; Saturated Fat: 1g; Sodium: 553mg; Total Carbohydrates: 38g; Dietary Fiber: 5g; Total Sugars: 5g; Protein: 8g

Quick-to-make Quesadillas

Servings: 4 | Prep Time: 20 Minutes | Cooking Time: 30 Minutes

Ingredients:

- 340 grams goat cheese
- 2 tbsp vinegar
- 1 tbsp Taco seasoning
- 1 ripe avocado, pitted
- 4 scallions, finely sliced
- 2 tbsp lemon juice
- 4 flour tortillas
- ¼ cup hot sauce
- ½ cup Alfredo sauce
- 16 cherry tomatoes, halved

Directions:

1. Preheat air fryer to 200°C/400°F.
2. Slice goat cheese into 4 pieces. Set aside. In a bowl, whisk vinegar and taco seasoning until combined. Submerge each slice into the vinegar and Air Fry for 12 minutes until crisp, turning once. Let cool slightly before cutting into 1-cm thick strips.
3. Using a fork, mash the avocado in a bowl. Stir in scallions

and lemon juice and set aside.

4. Lay one tortilla on a flat surface, cut from one edge to the center, then spread ¼ of the avocado mixture on one quadrant, 1 tbsp of hot sauce on the next quadrant, and finally 2 tbsp of Alfredo sauce on the other half. Top the non-sauce half with ¼ of cherry tomatoes and ¼ of goat cheese strips.
5. To fold, start with the avocado quadrant, folding each over the next one until you create a stacked triangle. Repeat the process with the remaining tortillas.
6. Air Fry for 5 minutes until crispy, turning once. Serve warm.

Variations & Ingredients Tips:

- Use feta cheese or queso fresco instead of goat cheese.
- Add sautéed bell peppers and onions to the filling.
- Serve with salsa, sour cream, or guacamole for dipping.

Per Serving: Calories: 500; Total Fat: 28g; Saturated Fat: 17g; Sodium: 1050mg; Total Carbohydrates: 42g; Dietary Fiber: 5g; Total Sugars: 6g; Protein: 22g

Vietnamese Gingered Tofu

Servings: 4 | Prep Time: 10 Minutes | Cooking Time: 25 Minutes

Ingredients:

- 1 package extra-firm tofu, cubed
- 4 tsp shoyu (soy sauce)
- 1 tsp onion powder
- 1/2 tsp garlic powder
- 1/2 tsp ginger powder
- 1/2 tsp turmeric powder
- Black pepper to taste
- 2 tbsp nutritional yeast
- 1 tsp dried rosemary
- 1 tsp dried dill
- 2 tsp cornstarch
- 2 tsp sunflower oil

Directions:

1. Sprinkle the tofu with shoyu and toss to coat.
2. Add the onion, garlic, ginger, turmeric, and pepper. Gently toss to coat.
3. Add the yeast, rosemary, dill, and cornstarch. Toss to coat.
4. Dribble with the oil and toss again.
5. Preheat air fryer to 200°C/390°F. Spray the basket with oil.
6. Put the tofu in the basket and Bake for 7 minutes.
7. Remove, shake gently, and cook for another 7 minutes or until crispy and golden.
8. Serve warm.

Variations & Ingredients Tips:

- Use tamari or coconut aminos instead of soy sauce.
- Add chili garlic sauce or sriracha for a spicy kick.
- Toss with chopped scallions before serving.

Per Serving: Calories: 132; Total Fat: 7g; Saturated Fat: 1g; Sodium: 514mg; Total Carbohydrates: 8g; Dietary Fiber: 2g; Total Sugars: 1g; Protein: 13g

Mushroom-rice Stuffed Bell Peppers

Servings: 4 | Prep Time: 20 Minutes | Cooking Time: 30 Minutes

Ingredients:

- 4 red bell peppers, tops sliced
- 1 ½ cups cooked rice
- ¼ cup chopped leeks
- ¼ cup sliced mushrooms
- ¾ cup tomato sauce
- Salt and pepper to taste
- ¾ cup shredded mozzarella
- 2 tbsp parsley, chopped

Directions:

1. Fill a large pot of water and heat on high until it boils. Remove seeds and membranes from the peppers. Carefully place peppers into the boiling water for 5 minutes. Remove and set aside to cool.
2. Mix together rice, leeks, mushrooms, tomato sauce, parsley, salt, and pepper in a large bowl. Stuff each pepper with the rice mixture. Top with mozzarella.
3. Preheat air fryer to 180°C/350°F. Arrange the peppers on the greased air fryer basket and Bake for 10 minutes. Serve.

Variations & Ingredients Tips:

- Use quinoa, couscous, or cauliflower rice instead of regular rice.
- Add ground veggie crumbles or lentils for more protein.
- Top with hot sauce or sriracha for a spicy touch.

Per Serving: Calories: 210; Total Fat: 6g; Saturated Fat: 3.5g; Sodium: 420mg; Total Carbohydrates: 29g; Dietary Fiber: 4g; Total Sugars: 8g; Protein: 11g

Asparagus, Mushroom And Cheese Soufflés

Servings: 3 | Prep Time: 20 Minutes | Cooking Time: 21 Minutes

Ingredients:

- butter
- grated Parmesan cheese
- 3 button mushrooms, thinly sliced
- 8 spears asparagus, sliced 1.25-cm long
- 1 teaspoon olive oil
- 1 tablespoon butter
- 4½ teaspoons flour
- pinch paprika
- pinch ground nutmeg
- salt and freshly ground black pepper
- ½ cup milk
- ½ cup grated Gruyère cheese or other Swiss cheese
- 2 eggs, separated

Directions:

1. Butter three 170-g ramekins and dust with grated Parmesan cheese. (Butter the ramekins and then coat the butter with Parmesan by shaking it around in the ramekin and dumping out any excess.)
2. Preheat the air fryer to 200°C/400°F.
3. Toss the mushrooms and asparagus in a bowl with the olive oil. Transfer the vegetables to the air fryer and air-fry for 7 minutes, shaking the basket once or twice to redistribute the ingredients while they cook.
4. While the vegetables are cooking, make the soufflé base. Melt the butter in a saucepan on the stovetop over medium heat. Add the flour, stir and cook for a minute or two. Add the paprika, nutmeg, salt and pepper. Whisk in the milk and bring the mixture to a simmer to thicken. Remove the pan from the heat and add the cheese, stirring to melt. Let the mixture cool for just a few minutes and then whisk the egg yolks in, one at a time. Stir in the cooked mushrooms and asparagus. Let this soufflé base cool.
5. In a separate bowl, whisk the egg whites to soft peak stage (the point at which the whites can almost stand up on the end of your whisk). Fold the whipped egg whites into the soufflé base, adding a little at a time.
6. Preheat the air fryer to 165°C/330°F.
7. Transfer the batter carefully to the buttered ramekins, leaving about 1.25-cm at the top. Place the ramekins into the air fryer basket and air-fry for 14 minutes. The soufflés should have risen nicely and be brown on top. Serve immediately.

Variations & Ingredients Tips:

- Use different vegetables like spinach, broccoli, or bell peppers for a variety of flavors.
- Substitute Gruyère with cheddar, gouda, or brie for a different cheese profile.
- Serve the soufflés with a side salad or crusty bread for a complete meal.

Per Serving (1 soufflé): Calories: 290; Cholesterol: 165mg; Total Fat: 20g; Saturated Fat: 11g; Sodium: 410mg; Total Carbohydrates: 12g; Dietary Fiber: 1g; Total Sugars: 4g; Protein: 16g

Spaghetti Squash And Kale Fritters With Pomodoro Sauce

Servings: 3 | Prep Time: 20 Minutes | Cooking Time: 45 Minutes

Ingredients:

- 680g spaghetti squash (about half a large or a whole small squash)
- Olive oil
- 1/2 onion, diced
- 1/2 red bell pepper, diced
- 2 cloves garlic, minced
- 4 cups coarsely chopped
- kale
- Salt and freshly ground black pepper
- 1 egg
- 1/3 cup breadcrumbs, divided*
- 1/3 cup grated Parmesan cheese
- 1/2 teaspoon dried

rubbed sage
- Pinch nutmeg
- 2 tablespoons olive oil
- 1/2 onion, chopped
- 1 to 2 cloves garlic, minced
- 1 (800g) can peeled tomatoes
- 1/4 cup red wine
- 1 teaspoon Italian seasoning
- 2 tablespoons chopped fresh basil, plus more for garnish
- Salt and freshly ground black pepper
- 1/2 teaspoon sugar (optional)

Directions:

1. Preheat the air fryer to 190°C/370°F.
2. Cut the spaghetti squash in half lengthwise and remove the seeds. Rub with olive oil and season with salt and pepper. Air fry for 30 minutes, flipping halfway.
3. Sauté onions, pepper, garlic and kale. Transfer to a bowl and let cool.
4. Make Pomodoro sauce: Sauté onion and garlic. Add tomatoes, wine, seasoning and basil. Simmer 20 mins. Season.
5. Scrape spaghetti squash flesh onto a sheet pan and let cool.
6. Add squash to kale mix with egg, breadcrumbs, cheese, spices and seasoning. Form 6 portions and brush with oil.
7. Air fry fritters at 190°C/370°F for 15 minutes, flipping halfway.
8. Serve fritters warm with Pomodoro sauce and garnish with basil.

Variations & Ingredients Tips:

- Substitute panko for regular breadcrumbs.
- Use plant-based parmesan for a vegan version.
- Add sun-dried tomatoes or olives to the fritter batter.

Per Serving: Calories: 389; Total Fat: 18g; Saturated Fat: 4g; Sodium: 585mg; Total Carbohydrates: 45g; Dietary Fiber: 7g; Total Sugars: 12g; Protein: 14g

Pizza Margherita With Spinach

Servings: 4 | Prep Time: 30 Minutes | Cooking Time: 50 Minutes

Ingredients:

- ½ cup pizza sauce
- 1 tsp dried oregano
- 1 tsp garlic powder
- 1 pizza dough
- 1 cup baby spinach
- ½ cup mozzarella cheese

Directions:

1. Preheat air fryer to 200°C/400°F.
2. Whisk pizza sauce, oregano, and garlic in a bowl. Set aside.
3. Form 4 balls with the pizza dough and roll out each into a 15-cm round pizza.
4. Lay one crust in the basket, spread ¼ of the sauce, then scatter with ¼ of spinach, and finally top with mozzarella cheese.
5. Grill for 8 minutes until golden brown and the crust is crispy.
6. Repeat the process with the remaining crusts. Serve immediately.

Variations & Ingredients Tips:

- Add sliced cherry tomatoes, mushrooms, or bell peppers as additional toppings.
- Sprinkle with red pepper flakes for some heat.
- Brush the crust with garlic butter before adding toppings for extra flavor.

Per Serving: Calories: 280; Total Fat: 9g; Saturated Fat: 3.5g; Sodium: 520mg; Total Carbohydrates: 39g; Dietary Fiber: 2g; Total Sugars: 4g; Protein: 11g

Desserts And Sweets

German Streusel-stuffed Baked Apples

Servings: 4 | Prep Time: 15 Minutes | Cooking Time: 40 Minutes

Ingredients:

- 2 large apples
- 3 tbsp flour
- 3 tbsp light brown sugar
- ⅛ tsp ground cinnamon
- 1 tsp vanilla extract
- 1 tsp chopped pecans
- 2 tbsp cold butter
- 2 tbsp salted caramel sauce

Directions:

1. Cut the apples in half through the stem and scoop out the core and seeds.
2. Mix flour, brown sugar, vanilla, pecans and cinnamon in a bowl. Cut in the butter with a fork until it turns into crumbs.
3. Top each apple half with 2 ½ tbsp of the crumble mixture.
4. Preheat air fryer to 165°C/325°F.
5. Put the apple halves in the greased air fryer basket. Cook until soft in the center and the crumble is golden, about 25-30 minutes.
6. Serve warm topped with caramel sauce.

Variations & Ingredients Tips:

- Use pears or peaches instead of apples.
- Add dried cranberries, raisins, or chopped dates to the streusel.
- Drizzle with melted white or dark chocolate in addition to the caramel.

Per Serving: Calories: 220; Total Fat: 10g; Saturated Fat: 5g; Sodium: 130mg; Total Carbohydrates: 34g; Dietary Fiber: 3g; Total Sugars: 25g; Protein: 1g

Oreo-coated Peanut Butter Cups

Servings: 8 | Prep Time: 20 Minutes | Cooking Time: 4 Minutes

Ingredients:

- 8 Standard 21-g peanut butter cups, frozen
- 1/3 cup all-purpose flour
- 2 large egg white(s), beaten until foamy
- 16 Oreos or other creme-filled chocolate sand-
- wich cookies, ground to crumbs in a food processor
- Vegetable oil spray

Directions:

1. Set up and fill three shallow plates on your counter: one for flour, one for beaten egg white(s), and one for cookie crumbs.
2. Dip a frozen peanut butter cup in flour, coating all sides. Shake off excess, then dip in egg white(s). Let excess drip off, then coat in cookie crumbs. Dip back in egg white(s) then cookie crumbs again, making sure it's evenly coated. Set aside and repeat with remaining cups.
3. Lightly spray the coated cups on all sides with oil. Set on a plate and freeze while preheating air fryer.
4. Preheat air fryer to 200°C/400°F.
5. Place cups wider side up in basket, leaving space between. Air-fry for 4 minutes until soft but coating is set.
6. Turn off and remove basket. Let sit 10 minutes, then use spatula to transfer to a wire rack. Cool at least 5 more minutes before serving.

Variations & Ingredients Tips:

- Use different flavored Oreos like mint, peanut butter or golden.
- Drizzle with melted chocolate or caramel after air frying.
- Crush candy canes and use in place of some of the cookie crumbs.

Per Serving: Calories: 310; Total Fat: 19g; Saturated Fat: 9g; Cholesterol: 5mg; Sodium: 180mg; Total Carbs: 33g; Dietary Fiber: 2g; Total Sugars: 22g; Protein: 5g

Home-style Pumpkin Pie Pudding

Servings: 4 | Prep Time: 10 Minutes | Cooking Time: 30 Minutes

Ingredients:

- 1 cup canned pumpkin purée
- 1/4 cup sugar
- 3 tbsp all-purpose flour
- 1 tbsp butter, melted
- 1 egg
- 1 orange, zested
- 2 tbsp milk
- 1 tsp vanilla extract
- 4 vanilla wafers, crumbled

Directions:

1. Preheat air fryer to 175°C/350°F.
2. Beat pumpkin, sugar, flour, butter, egg, orange zest, milk and vanilla until well-mixed.
3. Grease a baking pan and pour in pumpkin mixture.
4. Place pan in air fryer basket and bake for 11-17 minutes until golden brown.

5. Remove pudding and let it chill.
6. Serve topped with crumbled vanilla wafers.

Variations & Ingredients Tips:

- Use sweetened condensed milk for a richer pudding.
- Add warm spices like cinnamon, nutmeg and ginger.
- Top with whipped cream or marshmallows.

Per Serving: Calories: 178; Total Fat: 6g; Saturated Fat: 3g; Sodium: 103mg; Total Carbohydrates: 27g; Dietary Fiber: 2g; Total Sugars: 17g; Protein: 4g

Fried Oreos Recipes

Servings: 12 | Prep Time: 10 Minutes | Cooking Time: 6 Minutes Per Batch

Ingredients:

- oil for misting or non-stick spray
- 1 cup complete pancake and waffle mix
- 1 teaspoon vanilla extract
- ½ cup water, plus 2 tablespoons
- 12 Oreos or other chocolate sandwich cookies
- 1 tablespoon confectioners' sugar

Directions:

1. Spray baking pan with oil or nonstick spray and place in basket.
2. Preheat air fryer to 200°C/390°F.
3. In a medium bowl, mix together the pancake mix, vanilla, and water.
4. Dip 4 cookies in batter and place in baking pan.
5. Cook for 6 minutes, until browned.
6. Repeat steps 4 and 5 for the remaining cookies.
7. Sift sugar over warm cookies.

Variations & Ingredients Tips:

- Use different cookie flavors like golden Oreos, snickerdoodles, or chocolate chip.
- Mix in cocoa powder, cinnamon, or nutmeg into the batter for extra flavor.
- Top with a drizzle of chocolate ganache or a sprinkle of sea salt.

Per Serving: Calories: 140; Total Fat: 6g; Saturated Fat: 1.5g; Sodium: 170mg; Total Carbohydrates: 21g; Dietary Fiber: 0g; Total Sugars: 11g; Protein: 1g

Fried Cannoli Wontons

Servings: 10 | Prep Time: 20 Minutes | Cooking Time: 8 Minutes

Ingredients:

- 227 grams Neufchâtel cream cheese
- ¼ cup powdered sugar
- 1 teaspoon vanilla extract
- ¼ teaspoon salt
- ¼ cup mini chocolate chips
- 2 tablespoons chopped pecans (optional)
- 20 wonton wrappers
- ¼ cup filtered water

Directions:

1. Preheat the air fryer to 190°C/370°F.
2. In a large bowl, use a hand mixer to combine the cream cheese with the powdered sugar, vanilla, and salt. Fold in the chocolate chips and pecans. Set aside.
3. Lay the wonton wrappers out on a flat, smooth surface and place a bowl with the filtered water next to them.
4. Use a teaspoon to evenly divide the cream cheese mixture among the 20 wonton wrappers, placing the batter in the center of the wontons.
5. Wet the tip of your index finger, and gently moisten the outer edges of the wrapper. Then fold each wrapper until it creates a secure pocket.
6. Liberally spray the air fryer basket with olive oil mist.
7. Place the wontons into the basket, and cook for 5 to 8 minutes. When the outer edges begin to brown, remove the wontons from the air fryer basket. Repeat cooking with remaining wontons.
8. Serve warm.

Variations & Ingredients Tips:

- Use ricotta cheese or mascarpone instead of cream cheese for a more authentic flavor.
- Add a pinch of cinnamon or orange zest to the filling.
- Dust with powdered sugar or drizzle with chocolate sauce before serving.

Per Serving: Calories: 140; Total Fat: 8g; Saturated Fat: 4g; Sodium: 200mg; Total Carbohydrates: 14g; Dietary Fiber: 0g; Total Sugars: 5g; Protein: 4g

Apple Dumplings

Servings: 4 | Prep Time: 20 Minutes | Cooking Time: 25 Minutes

Ingredients:

- 1 Basic Pie Dough (see the following recipe)
- 4 medium Granny Smith or Pink Lady apples, peeled and cored
- 4 tablespoons sugar
- 4 teaspoons cinnamon
- 1/2 teaspoon ground nutmeg
- 4 tablespoons unsalted butter, melted
- 4 scoops ice cream, for serving

Directions:

1. Preheat the air fryer to 165°C/330°F.
2. Bring the pie crust recipe to room temperature.
3. Place the pie crust on a floured surface. Divide the dough

into 4 equal pieces. Roll out each piece to 0.6cm-thick rounds.

4. Place an apple onto each dough round. Sprinkle 1 tablespoon of sugar in the core part of each apple; sprinkle 1 teaspoon cinnamon and 1/8 teaspoon nutmeg over each. Place 1 tablespoon of butter into the center of each.
5. Fold up the sides and fully cover the cored apples.
6. Place the dumplings into the air fryer basket and spray with cooking spray. Cook for 25 minutes. Check after 14 minutes cooking; if they're getting too brown, reduce the heat to 160°C/320°F and complete the cooking.
7. Serve hot apple dumplings with a scoop of ice cream.

Variations & Ingredients Tips:

- Use different apple varieties like Honeycrisp or Fuji.
- Add raisins or chopped nuts to the filling.
- Drizzle with caramel sauce before serving.

Per Serving: Calories: 375; Total Fat: 18g; Saturated Fat: 10g; Sodium: 195mg; Total Carbohydrates: 51g; Dietary Fiber: 4g; Total Sugars: 29g; Protein: 3g

Honey-pecan Yogurt Cake

Servings: 6 | Prep Time: 15 Minutes | Cooking Time: 18-24 Minutes

Ingredients:

- 1 cup plus 3 1/2 tablespoons All-purpose flour
- 1/4 teaspoon Baking powder
- 1/4 teaspoon Baking soda
- 1/4 teaspoon Table salt
- 5 tablespoons Plain
- Greek yogurt
- 5 tablespoons Honey
- 5 tablespoons Egg substitute
- 2 teaspoons Vanilla extract
- 2/3 cup Chopped pecans
- Baking spray

Directions:

1. Preheat air fryer to 165°C/325°F (or 170°C/330°F).
2. Mix flour, baking powder, soda and salt.
3. Beat yogurt, honey, egg substitute and vanilla until smooth.
4. Fold in flour mix just until moistened. Fold in pecans.
5. Grease a 15cm, 18cm or 20cm round cake pan. Spread batter evenly.
6. Bake for 18 mins (15cm), 22 mins (18cm), 24 mins (20cm) until toothpick comes out clean.
7. Cool in pan 5 mins, then unmold and let cool completely before slicing.

Variations & Ingredients Tips:

- Use maple syrup instead of honey.
- Add spices like cinnamon, nutmeg or cardamom.
- Top with cream cheese frosting and extra pecans.

Per Serving: Calories: 266; Total Fat: 11g; Saturated Fat: 2g; Sodium: 227mg; Total Carbohydrates: 37g; Dietary Fiber: 2g;

Total Sugars: 14g; Protein: 6g

Baked Stuffed Pears

Servings: 4 | Prep Time: 15 Minutes | Cooking Time: 15 Minutes + Cooling Time

Ingredients:

- 4 cored pears, halved
- 1/2 cup chopped cashews
- 1/2 cup dried cranberries
- 1/4 cup agave nectar
- 1/2 stick butter, softened
- 1/2 tsp ground cinnamon
- 1/2 cup apple juice

Directions:

1. Preheat the air fryer to 180°C/350°F.
2. Combine the cashews, cranberries, agave nectar, butter, and cinnamon and mix well.
3. Stuff this mixture into the pears, heaping it up on top.
4. Set the pears in a baking pan and pour the apple juice into the bottom of the pan.
5. Put the pan in the fryer and Bake for 10-12 minutes or until the pears are tender.
6. Let cool before serving.

Variations & Ingredients Tips:

- Use honey or maple syrup instead of agave nectar.
- Add chopped dates or raisins to the stuffing mixture.
- Sprinkle with cinnamon sugar before baking.

Per Serving: Calories: 370; Total Fat: 19g; Saturated Fat: 7g; Sodium: 83mg; Total Carbohydrates: 51g; Dietary Fiber: 7g; Total Sugars: 36g; Protein: 5g

Wild Blueberry Sweet Empanadas

Servings: 12 | Prep Time: 30 Minutes (includes Chilling Jam) | Cooking Time: 8 Minutes

Ingredients:

- 2 cups frozen wild blueberries
- 5 tablespoons chia seeds
- 1/4 cup honey
- 1 tablespoon lemon or lime juice
- 1/4 cup water
- 1 1/2 cups all-purpose flour
- 1 cup whole-wheat flour
- 1/2 teaspoon salt
- 1 tablespoon sugar
- 1/2 cup cold unsalted butter
- 1 egg
- 1/2 cup plus 2 tablespoons milk, divided
- 1 cup powdered sugar
- 1 teaspoon vanilla extract

Directions:

1. To make the wild blueberry chia jam, place the blueberries, chia seeds, honey, lemon or lime juice, and water into a blender and pulse for 2 minutes. Pour the chia jam into a

glass jar or bowl and cover. Store in the refrigerator at least 4 to 8 hours or until the jam is thickened.

2. In a food processor, place the all-purpose flour, whole-wheat flour, salt, sugar, and butter and process for 2 minutes, scraping down the sides of the food processor every 30 seconds. Add in the egg and blend for 30 seconds. Using the pulse button, add in 1/2 cup of the milk 1 tablespoon at a time or until the dough is moist enough to handle and be rolled into a ball. Let the dough rest at room temperature for 30 minutes.

3. On a floured surface, cut the dough in half; then form a ball and cut each ball into 6 equal pieces, totaling 12 equal pieces. Work with one piece at a time, and cover the remaining dough with a towel. Roll out the dough into a 15cm round, with 6mm thickness. Place 4 tablespoons of filling in the center of round, fold over to form a half-circle. Using a fork, crimp the edges together and pierce the top with a fork for air holes. Repeat with the remaining dough and filling.

4. Preheat the air fryer to 175°C/350°F.

5. Working in batches, place 3 to 4 empanadas in the air fryer basket and spray with cooking spray. Cook for 8 minutes. Repeat in batches, as needed. Allow the sweet empanadas to cool for 15 minutes.

6. Meanwhile, in a small bowl, whisk together the powdered sugar, the remaining 2 tablespoons of milk, and the vanilla extract. Then drizzle the glaze over the surface and serve.

Variations & Ingredients Tips:

- Use other berry varieties like raspberries or blackberries.
- Dust with cinnamon-sugar before baking.
- Serve with vanilla ice cream or whipped cream.

Per Serving (1 empanada): Calories: 265; Total Fat: 11g; Saturated Fat: 6g; Cholesterol: 35mg; Sodium: 115mg; Total Carbs: 39g; Dietary Fiber: 4g; Total Sugars: 16g; Protein: 5g

Cinnamon Tortilla Crisps

Servings: 4 | Prep Time: 5 Minutes | Cooking Time: 8 Minutes

Ingredients:

- 1 tortilla
- 2 tsp muscovado sugar
- 1/2 tsp cinnamon

Directions:

1. Preheat air fryer to 175°C/350°F.
2. Slice tortilla into 8 triangles.
3. Spray tortilla triangles with oil on both sides.
4. Sprinkle with muscovado sugar and cinnamon.
5. Lightly spray tops with more oil.
6. Place in a single layer in air fryer basket.
7. Air Fry for 5-6 minutes until light brown.
8. Serve warm.

Variations & Ingredients Tips:

- Use a cinnamon-sugar mixture instead of separate ingredients.
- Add a pinch of cayenne for a kick of heat.
- Drizzle with honey or agave after cooking.

Per Serving: Calories: 66; Total Fat: 2g; Saturated Fat: 0g; Sodium: 88mg; Total Carbohydrates: 12g; Dietary Fiber: 1g; Total Sugars: 3g; Protein: 1g

Sea-salted Caramel Cookie Cups

Servings: 12 | Prep Time: 10 Minutes | Cooking Time: 12 Minutes

Ingredients:

- 1/3 cup butter
- 1/4 cup brown sugar
- 1 teaspoon vanilla extract
- 1 large egg
- 1 cup all-purpose flour
- 1/2 cup old-fashioned
- oats
- 1/2 teaspoon baking soda
- 1/4 teaspoon salt
- 1/3 cup sea-salted caramel chips

Directions:

1. Preheat the air fryer to 150°C/300°F.
2. In a large bowl, cream the butter with the brown sugar and vanilla. Whisk in the egg and set aside.
3. In a separate bowl, mix the flour, oats, baking soda, and salt. Then gently mix the dry ingredients into the wet. Fold in the caramel chips.
4. Divide the batter into 12 silicon muffin liners. Place the cookie cups into the air fryer basket and cook for 12 minutes or until a toothpick inserted in the center comes out clean.
5. Remove and let cool 5 minutes before serving.

Variations & Ingredients Tips:

- Use chocolate chips or white chocolate chips instead of caramel chips.
- Add chopped nuts like pecans or walnuts to the batter.
- Drizzle with extra caramel sauce after baking.

Per Serving: Calories: 160; Total Fat: 7g; Saturated Fat: 4g; Cholesterol: 30mg; Sodium: 150mg; Total Carbs: 22g; Dietary Fiber: 1g; Total Sugars: 10g; Protein: 2g

Roasted Pears

Servings: 4 | Prep Time: 5 Minutes | Cooking Time: 10 Minutes

Ingredients:

- 2 Ripe pears, preferably Anjou, stemmed, peeled, halved lengthwise, and
- cored
- 2 tablespoons Butter, melted

| 2 teaspoons Granulated white sugar | 1/4 cup Honey |
| Grated nutmeg | 1/2 cup (about 30g) Shaved Parmesan cheese |

Directions:

1. Preheat the air fryer to 200°C/400°F.
2. Brush each pear half with about 5ml of the melted butter, then sprinkle their cut sides with 1/2 teaspoon sugar. Grate a pinch of nutmeg over each pear.
3. When the machine is at temperature, set the pear halves cut side up in the basket with as much air space between them as possible. Air-fry undisturbed for 10 minutes, or until hot and softened.
4. Use a nonstick-safe spatula, and perhaps a flatware tablespoon for balance, to transfer the pear halves to a serving platter or plates. Cool for a minute or two, then drizzle each pear half with 1 tablespoon of the honey. Lay about 2 tablespoons of shaved Parmesan over each half just before serving.

Variations & Ingredients Tips:

- Use maple syrup instead of honey.
- Sprinkle with cinnamon instead of nutmeg.
- Top with chopped toasted nuts like almonds or pecans.

Per Serving: Calories: 190; Total Fat: 9g; Saturated Fat: 5g; Cholesterol: 20mg; Sodium: 130mg; Total Carbs: 27g; Dietary Fiber: 3g; Total Sugars: 21g; Protein: 3g

Cinnamon Canned Biscuit Donuts

Servings: 4 | Prep Time: 10 Minutes | Cooking Time: 25 Minutes

Ingredients:

- 1 can jumbo biscuits
- 1 cup cinnamon sugar

Directions:

1. Preheat air fryer to 180°C/360°F.
2. Separate biscuits into 8 pieces and cut a hole in the center of each.
3. Place 4 biscuit donuts in the air fryer basket. Spray with oil.
4. Bake for 8 minutes, flipping once halfway.
5. While still warm, coat donuts in cinnamon sugar mixture.
6. Serve immediately.

Variations & Ingredients Tips:

- Use a glaze or powdered sugar coating instead of cinnamon sugar.
- Fill the centers with fruit jam or chocolate hazelnut spread.
- Drizzle with melted butter before coating in cinnamon sugar.

Per Serving (2 donuts): Calories: 262; Total Fat: 6g; Saturat-

ed Fat: 1g; Sodium: 469mg; Total Carbohydrates: 51g; Dietary Fiber: 1g; Total Sugars: 24g; Protein: 4g

Healthy Chickpea Cookies

Servings: 6 | Prep Time: 15 Minutes | Cooking Time: 25 Minutes

Ingredients:

- 1 cup canned chickpeas
- 2 tsp vanilla extract
- 1 tsp lemon juice
- 1/3 cup date paste
- 2 tbsp butter, melted
- 1/3 cup flour
- 1/2 tsp baking powder
- 1/4 cup dark chocolate chips

Directions:

1. Preheat air fryer to 160°C/320°F. Line the basket with parchment paper.
2. In a blender, blend chickpeas, vanilla, and lemon juice until smooth. Transfer to a bowl.
3. Stir in date paste and melted butter until well combined.
4. Mix in flour, baking powder, and chocolate chips.
5. Scoop 2-tablespoon portions and shape into balls.
6. Place balls on the parchment and flatten slightly into cookie shapes.
7. Bake for 13 minutes until golden brown.
8. Let cool slightly before serving.

Variations & Ingredients Tips:

- Use mashed banana or applesauce instead of date paste.
- Substitute nut butter for the regular butter.
- Add nuts, dried fruit, or seeds to the batter.

Per Serving (2 cookies): Calories: 168; Total Fat: 6g; Saturated Fat: 3g; Sodium: 134mg; Total Carbohydrates: 25g; Dietary Fiber: 3g; Total Sugars: 9g; Protein: 4g

Easy Churros

Servings: 12 | Prep Time: 30 Minutes | Cooking Time: 10 Minutes

Ingredients:

- ½ cup Water
- 4 tablespoons (¼ cup/½ stick) Butter
- ¼ teaspoon Table salt
- ½ cup All-purpose flour
- 2 Large egg(s)
- ¼ cup Granulated white sugar
- 2 teaspoons Ground cinnamon

Directions:

1. Bring the water, butter, and salt to a boil in a small saucepan set over high heat, stirring occasionally.
2. When the butter has fully melted, reduce the heat to medium and stir in the flour to form a dough. Continue cooking.

stirring constantly, to dry out the dough until it coats the bottom and sides of the pan with a film, even a crust. Remove the pan from the heat, scrape the dough into a bowl, and cool for 15 minutes.

3. Using an electric hand mixer at medium speed, beat in the egg, or eggs one at a time, until the dough is smooth and firm enough to hold its shape.

4. Mix the sugar and cinnamon in a small bowl. Scoop up 1 tablespoon of the dough and roll it in the sugar mixture to form a small, coated tube about 1-cm in diameter and 5-cm long. Set it aside and make 5 more tubes for the small batch or 11 more for the large one.

5. Set the tubes on a plate and freeze for 20 minutes. Meanwhile, Preheat the air fryer to 190°C/375°F.

6. Set 3 frozen tubes in the basket for a small batch or 6 for a large one with as much air space between them as possible. Air-fry undisturbed for 10 minutes, or until puffed, brown, and set.

7. Use kitchen tongs to transfer the churros to a wire rack to cool for at least 5 minutes. Meanwhile, air-fry and cool the second batch of churros in the same way.

Variations & Ingredients Tips:

- Dip the cooled churros in melted chocolate or caramel sauce.
- Pipe the dough into different shapes like rings, hearts, or stars.
- Serve with hot chocolate or coffee for dunking.

Per Serving: Calories: 110; Total Fat: 5g; Saturated Fat: 3g; Sodium: 80mg; Total Carbohydrates: 14g; Dietary Fiber: 0g; Total Sugars: 7g; Protein: 2g

Cheesecake Wontons

Servings: 16 | Prep Time: 20 Minutes | Cooking Time: 6 Minutes

Ingredients:

- 1/4 cup Regular or low-fat cream cheese (not fat-free)
- 2 tablespoons Granulated white sugar
- 1 1/2 tablespoons Egg yolk
- 1/4 teaspoon Vanilla extract
- 1/8 teaspoon Table salt
- 1 1/2 tablespoons All-purpose flour
- 16 Wonton wrappers (vegetarian, if a concern)
- Vegetable oil spray

Directions:

1. Preheat air fryer to 200°C/400°F.
2. Mash cream cheese, sugar, egg yolk, vanilla and salt until smooth.
3. Add flour and mash until fully combined.
4. Place 1 tsp filling in center of a wonton wrapper. Wet edges and fold into a triangle, sealing edges.
5. Fold side corners over filling and press to seal into a

wonton shape.
6. Repeat with remaining wrappers and filling.
7. Mist wontons with oil spray on all sides.
8. Air fry for 6 minutes until golden brown and crisp.
9. Transfer to a wire rack and cool 5 minutes before serving.

Variations & Ingredients Tips:

- Add lemon or orange zest to the cheesecake filling.
- Brush with melted butter instead of oil spray.
- Serve with berry compote or chocolate sauce for dipping.

Per Serving (2 wontons): Calories: 66; Total Fat: 3g; Saturated Fat: 1g; Sodium: 65mg; Total Carbohydrates: 8g; Dietary Fiber: 0g; Total Sugars: 2g; Protein: 2g

Holiday Peppermint Cake

Servings: 4 | Prep Time: 10 Minutes | Cooking Time: 20 Minutes

Ingredients:

- 1 1/2 cups flour
- 3 eggs
- 1/3 cup molasses
- 1/2 cup olive oil
- 1/2 cup almond milk
- 1/2 tsp vanilla extract
- 1/2 tsp peppermint extract
- 1 tsp baking powder
- 1/2 tsp salt

Directions:

1. Preheat air fryer to 190°C/380°F.
2. Whisk the eggs and molasses until smooth.
3. Slowly mix in olive oil, almond milk, vanilla and peppermint extracts
4. In another bowl, sift together flour, baking powder and salt.
5. Gradually incorporate dry ingredients into wet ingredients until combined.
6. Pour batter into a greased baking pan and place in air fryer basket.
7. Bake for 12-15 minutes until a toothpick inserted comes out clean.
8. Serve and enjoy!

Variations & Ingredients Tips:

- Use coconut or vegetable oil instead of olive oil.
- Add crushed peppermint candies or chocolate chips to the batter.
- Top with peppermint frosting or whipped cream.

Per Serving: Calories: 538; Total Fat: 27g; Saturated Fat: 4g; Sodium: 307mg; Total Carbohydrates: 67g; Dietary Fiber: 2g; Total Sugars: 28g; Protein: 8g

Fried Pineapple Chunks

Servings: 3 | Prep Time: 20 Minutes | Cooking Time: 10 Minutes

Ingredients:

- 3 tablespoons Corn-starch
- 1 Large egg white, beaten until foamy
- 1 cup (113 grams) Ground vanilla wafer cookies (not low-fat cookies)
- ¼ teaspoon Ground dried ginger
- 18 (about 2¼ cups) Fresh 2.5-cm chunks peeled and cored pineapple

Directions:

1. Preheat the air fryer to 200°C/400°F.
2. Put the cornstarch in a medium or large bowl. Put the beaten egg white in a small bowl. Pour the cookie crumbs and ground dried ginger into a large zip-closed plastic bag, shaking it a bit to combine them.
3. Dump the pineapple chunks into the bowl with the cornstarch. Toss and stir until well coated. Use your cleaned fingers or a large fork like a shovel to pick up a few pineapple chunks, shake off any excess cornstarch, and put them in the bowl with the egg white. Stir gently, then pick them up and let any excess egg white slip back into the rest. Put them in the bag with the crumb mixture. Repeat the cornstarch-then-egg process until all the pineapple chunks are in the bag. Seal the bag and shake gently, turning the bag this way and that, to coat the pieces well.
4. Set the coated pineapple chunks in the basket with as much air space between them as possible. Even a fraction of 0.25 cm will work, but they should not touch. Air-fry undisturbed for 10 minutes, or until golden brown and crisp.
5. Gently dump the contents of the basket onto a wire rack. Cool for at least 5 minutes or up to 15 minutes before serving.

Variations & Ingredients Tips:

- Substitute pineapple with mango, papaya, or apple chunks.
- Use cinnamon, nutmeg, or cardamom instead of ginger for different spice flavors.
- Serve with a scoop of coconut ice cream or a drizzle of rum caramel sauce.

Per Serving: Calories: 320; Total Fat: 12g; Saturated Fat: 3.5g; Sodium: 170mg; Total Carbohydrates: 50g; Dietary Fiber: 2g; Total Sugars: 30g; Protein: 4g

Keto Cheesecake Cups

Servings: 6 | Prep Time: 10 Minutes | Cooking Time: 10 Minutes

Ingredients:

- 225-g cream cheese
- 1/4 cup plain whole-milk Greek yogurt
- 1 large egg
- 1 teaspoon pure vanilla extract
- 3 tablespoons monk fruit sweetener
- 1/4 teaspoon salt
- 1/2 cup walnuts, roughly chopped

Directions:

1. Preheat the air fryer to 155°C/315°F.
2. Beat the cream cheese with yogurt, egg, vanilla, sweetener and salt until combined.
3. Fold in the chopped walnuts.
4. Fill 6 silicone muffin liners with the batter. Place in an air fryer pan.
5. Carefully put the pan in the air fryer basket and cook for 10 minutes until lightly browned.
6. Refrigerate the cheesecake cups for 3 hours before serving.

Variations & Ingredients Tips:

- Use other keto-friendly sweeteners like erythritol or stevia.
- Add lemon or orange zest to the batter.
- Top with fresh berries or sugar-free chocolate syrup.

Per Serving: Calories: 205; Total Fat: 18g; Saturated Fat: 9g; Sodium: 166mg; Total Carbohydrates: 4g; Dietary Fiber: 1g; Total Sugars: 2g; Protein: 6g

Kiwi Pastry Bites

Servings: 6 | Prep Time: 15 Minutes | Cooking Time: 45 Minutes

Ingredients:

- 3 kiwi fruits, cut into 12 pieces
- 12 wonton wrappers
- 1/2 cup peanut butter

Directions:

1. Lay wonton wrappers on a flat surface.
2. Place a kiwi piece on each wrapper, then 1 tsp peanut butter.
3. Fold wrapper into a triangle, bringing bottom corners together but not sealing.
4. Press out air and seal open edges.
5. Preheat air fryer to 190°C/370°F.
6. Bake wontons in greased basket for 15-18 minutes, flipping halfway, until golden.
7. Let cool for a few minutes before serving.

Variations & Ingredients Tips:

- Use other fruits like apple, peach or mango slices.
- Substitute almond or cashew butter for peanut.
- Brush wontons with an egg wash before baking for a shiny finish.

Per Serving (2 pastry bites): Calories: 134; Total Fat: 7g; Saturated Fat: 1g; Sodium: 115mg; Total Carbohydrates: 16g; Dietary Fiber: 2g; Total Sugars: 6g; Protein: 4g

INDEX

A

Apple Dumplings   77
Apple French Toast Sandwich   14
Asian Glazed Meatballs   51
Asian-style Orange Chicken   39
Asparagus, Mushroom And Cheese Soufflés   74
Authentic Country-style Pork Ribs   22

B

Bacon, Blue Cheese And Pear Stuffed Pork Chops   21
Baked Shishito Peppers   64
Baked Stuffed Pears   78
Baltimore Crab Cakes   31
Barbecue Country-style Pork Ribs   25
Basil Mushroom & Shrimp Spaghetti   30
Best-ever Roast Beef Sandwiches   46
Bite-sized Blooming Onions   71
Black Bean Empanadas   68
Black Bean Stuffed Potato Boats   71
Black Bean Veggie Burgers   49
Breakfast Sausage Bites   12
Brie-currant & Bacon Spread   55
Brown Rice And Goat Cheese Croquettes   63
Buttered Brussels Sprouts   64
Buttered Chicken Thighs   42

C

Caponata Salsa   53
Caraway Seed Pretzel Sticks   64
Carrots & Parsnips With Tahini Sauce   61
Charred Shishito Peppers   60
Cheddar-pimiento Strips | Prep Time: 15 Minutes | Servings: 4   54
Cheesecake Wontons   81
Cheesy Mushroom-stuffed Pork Loins   22
Cheesy Pigs In A Blanket   53
Cheesy Texas Toast   67
Cheesy Tortellini Bites   60
Chicken & Fruit Biryani   37

Chicken Apple Brie Melt   52
Chicken Eggrolls   66
Chicken Fried Steak   16
Chicken Gyros   52
Chicken Parmigiana   40
Chicken Saltimbocca Sandwiches   46
Chicken Spiedies   48
Chile Con Carne Galette   17
Chili Cheese Dogs   47
Christmas Chicken & Roasted Grape Salad   43
Christmas Eggnog Bread   12
Cinnamon Canned Biscuit Donuts   80
Cinnamon Tortilla Crisps   79
Citrus Pork Lettuce Wraps   24
Classic Chicken Cobb Salad   42
Classic Crab Cakes   26
Coconut & Peanut Rice Cereal   10
Coconut Shrimp With Plum Sauce   34
Coffee-rubbed Pork Tenderloin   17
Corn Au Gratin   61
Corn Dog Bites   54
Crispy Chicken Bites With Gorgonzola Sauce   54
Crunchy Falafel Balls   49
Crunchy Fried Pork Loin Chops   22

D

Delicious Juicy Pork Meatballs   25
Dijon Thyme Burgers   45
Dill Fried Pickles With Light Ranch Dip   57

E

Easy Churros   80
Egg & Bacon Pockets   14
Egg Stuffed Pork Meatballs   17
Eggplant Parmesan Subs   46
Enchilada Chicken Quesadillas   41
English Scones   11

F

Fake Shepherd's Pie   72
Fiery Chicken Meatballs   43

Fish Goujons With Tartar Sauce   36
Fish Sticks For Grown-ups   35
Flank Steak With Chimichurri Sauce   18
Florentine Stuffed Tomatoes   62
Flounder Fillets   34
Fluffy Vegetable Strata   14
Fried Cannoli Wontons   77
Fried Goat Cheese   56
Fried Oreos Recipes   77
Fried Pineapple Chunks   81
Friendly Bbq Baby Back Ribs   18

G

Garlicky Brussel Sprouts With Saffron Aioli   71
German Streusel-stuffed Baked Apples   76
German-style Pork Patties   26
Golden Breaded Mushrooms   69
Greek Pita Pockets   25
Ground Beef Calzones   18

H

Healthy Chickpea Cookies   80
Healthy Granola   10
Herb-crusted Sole   28
Herby Prawn & Zucchini Bake   26
Hole In One   9
Holiday Lobster Salad   27
Holiday Peppermint Cake   81
Home Fries   65
Home-style Pumpkin Pie Pudding   76
Homemade Pretzel Bites   59
Honey-pecan Yogurt Cake   78
Horseradish Crusted Salmon   28
Horseradish Tuna Croquettes   28
Hot Cauliflower Bites   55
Huevos Rancheros   10

I

Indian Cauliflower Tikka Bites   58
Indian Chicken Tandoori   40
Indian Fry Bread Tacos   20
Inside-out Cheeseburgers   49
Intense Buffalo Chicken Wings   38
Italian Sausage Rolls   19

K

Kawaii Pork Roast   23

Kentucky-style Pork Tenderloin   21
Keto Cheesecake Cups   82
Kielbasa Sausage With Pierogies And Caramelized Onions   15
Kiwi Pastry Bites   82

L

Lamb Burgers   51
Lamb Meatballs With Quick Tomato Sauce   16
Lemon & Herb Crusted Salmon   33
Lollipop Lamb Chops With Mint Pesto   15

M

Mahi Mahi With Cilantro-chili Butter   32
Masala Fish `n´ Chips   29
Mediterranean Potato Skins   58
Mediterranean Salmon Burgers   34
Mexican Cheeseburgers   47
Mexican Chicken Roll-ups   41
Mexican-inspired Chicken Breasts   37
Mini Hasselback Potatoes   62
Miso-rubbed Salmon Fillets   29
Mixed Berry Muffins   9
Mom´s Tuna Melt Toastie   30
Mushroom-rice Stuffed Bell Peppers   74
Mustard-crusted Rib-eye   20

O

Oat Bran Muffins   12
Oktoberfest Bratwursts   23
Orange-glazed Carrots   59
Oreo-coated Peanut Butter Cups   76

P

Panko-breaded Cod Fillets   29
Paprika Fried Beef   23
Parmesan Portobello Mushroom Caps   69
Party Giant Nachos   70
Peach Fritters   8
Perfect Soft-shelled Crabs   33
Philly Cheesesteak Sandwiches   50
Pizza Margherita With Spinach   75
Popcorn Chicken Bites   55
Provolone Stuffed Meatballs   44

Q

Quick Tuna Tacos   34

Quick-to-make Quesadillas   73
Quinoa Green Pizza   70

R

Reuben Sandwiches   48
Rib Eye Cheesesteaks With Fried Onions   24
Rich Turkey Burgers   41
Roasted Herbed Shiitake Mushrooms   66
Roasted Pears   79
Roasted Tomato And Cheddar Rolls   9

S

Salmon Burgers   50
Saucy Shrimp   31
Sausage And Pepper Heros   44
Sea-salted Caramel Cookie Cups   79
Seedy Bagels   8
Shrimp "scampi"   27
Shrimp Po'boy With Remoulade Sauce   33
Shrimp, Chorizo And Fingerling Potatoes   35
Simple Buttermilk Fried Chicken   37
Simple Peppared Carrot Chips   62
Smoked Salmon Croissant Sandwich   13
Southern Okra Chips   64
Spaghetti Squash And Kale Fritters With Pomodoro
Sauce   74
Spiced Chicken Breasts   38
Spicy Fish Street Tacos With Sriracha Slaw   27
Spicy Hoisin Bbq Pork Chops   19
Spinach & Turkey Meatballs   42
Spinach And Cheese Calzone   68
Strawberry Streusel Muffins   13
Stuffed Shrimp   32
Stunning Apples & Onions   66
Succulent Roasted Peppers   66
Super-simple Herby Turkey   40

Sweet Potato Curly Fries   63
Sweet Potato Fries With Sweet And Spicy Dipping
Sauce   56
Sweet Potato Puffs   65
Sweet Potato–wrapped Shrimp   36
Sweet-and-salty Pretzels   56

T

Tacos   70
Taquitos   38
Tempura Fried Veggies   57
Tex-mex Beef Carnitas   21
Thyme Meatless Patties   72
Tilapia Teriyaki   31
Tortilla Crusted Chicken Breast   39
Turkey Scotch Eggs   39

V

Vegan Buddha Bowls   69
Veggie Fried Rice   72
Veggie Fritters   63
Vietnamese Beef Lettuce Wraps   19
Vietnamese Gingered Tofu   73

W

Walnut Pancake   13
Western Frittata   11
Western Omelet   8
White Bean Veggie Burgers   45
Wild Blueberry Sweet Empanadas   78

Y

Yellow Onion Rings   58
Yellow Squash   61
Yummy Salmon Burgers With Salsa Rosa   30

Printed in Great Britain
by Amazon

62777461R00051